ENZO ANGELUCCI   PAOLO MATRICARDI

COMBAT AIRCRAFT
OF WORLD WAR II
1943-1944

Illustrations by Pierluigi Pinto

a Salamander book

Published by Salamander Books Limited
LONDON ● NEW YORK

Created by Adriano Zannino
Editorial assistant Serenella Genoese Zerbi
Editor: Maria Luisa Ficarra
Translated from the Italian by Ruth Taylor

Consultant for color plate Bruno Benvenuti

Published by Salamander Books Ltd,
52 Bedford Row,
London WC1R 4LR
United Kingdom

ISBN 0 86101 417 0

Distributed in the UK by
Hodder & Stoughton Services,
P.O. Box 6,
Mill Road,
Dunton Green,
Sevenoaks,
Kent TN3 2XX

Printed in Italy by SAGDOS S.p.A., Milan

All correspondence concerning the contents of
this volume should be addressed to
Salamander Books Ltd.

THE TWO-ENGINE HEAVY FIGHTER

The structure of the modern monoplane fighter was definitively developed during the 1930s. The first aircraft in this category, produced by Germany and Great Britain, established a reference point to which eventually, all the major aeronautical powers conformed. Great speed, easy maneuverability and powerful armament were its main assets. These characteristics, fundamental in individual combat, nevertheless proved to be increasingly inadequate as the conflict continued. This was due to rapid changes in the conditions in the principal theaters of war. The appearance of faster and better armed bombers, and the intensification of strategic bombing missions upon targets thousands of miles away soon led to the need to integrate and strengthen the interceptor's traditional role. Thus the two-engine heavy fighter, a new class of combat planes, came into being. It was also usually a multi-seater, with only a few important exceptions. The inevitable decrease in overall performance in terms of speed and maneuverability was fully compensated for by a much greater range and heavier armament. The evolution of these aircraft led directly to the night fighters, a speciality that developed rapidly, especially in the European theater of war.

During World War II, the heavy fighter sector was pursued primarily by Germany, Great Britain, and the United States. In the remaining countries, the development of these aircraft was marginal or even non-existent, as in the case of Italy. Let us briefly examine the principal types: those that had an intensive career or that in some way contributed to the most significant evolutionary phases. In 1934, Germany was the first to design a long-range heavy fighter, intended as a bomber escort. This was the Messerschmitt Bf.110, also known as the famous *Zerstörer* (Destroyer). Its construction had been encouraged by Goering himself. However, this aircraft did not live up to expectations. Its trial by fire was the Battle of Britain, in which, faced with the fast and agile Spitfires and Hurricanes, Willy Messerschmitt's two-engine aircraft proved to be painfully awkward and indefensible. Nevertheless, once the limitations of its design had been recognized, the Bf.110 remained an irreplaceable weapon in the Luftwaffe's arsenal. Apart from its use as fighter-bomber and reconnaissance plane, it reached its element in the role of night fighter. In this speciality, its success was remarkable, and its employment reached a peak at the beginning of 1944, when 60 percent of the Luftwaffe's night fighters were Messerschmitt Bf.110s.

The Bf.110's failure as a conventional heavy fighter did not however impede the development of its successors, the Messerschmitt Me.210s and Me.410s. Although generally more advanced than the previous model (especially in their armament), both of these aircraft proved to be failures. The production of the Me.210 was suspended in April 1942, after barely 200 had been completed; the Me.410 was never outstanding, and, more to the point, it never proved to be very superior to the more reliable Bf.110 which it was supposed to replace.

Created right from the start as heavy fighters, Germany sent into action specifically as night fighters numerous adaptations of its most effective two-engine bombers (such as the Junkers Ju.88 and the Dornier Do.217). Afterwards it began building the Heinkel He.219, its most prestigious aircraft of all. Still judged today as the best aircraft in this category to serve in the Luftwaffe during World War II, this fast and powerful combat plane would perhaps have had a greater impact on the course of the war, if it had been available in greater numbers.

Apart from the unsuccessful Westland Whirlwind of 1940, (the RAF's first two-engine single-seater fighter) there were undoubtedly two protagonists in this category in Great Britain: the de Havilland Mosquito and the Bristol Beaufighter. The Mosquito, unanimously recognized as one of the most efficient and versatile combat planes of the entire war, has deservedly acquired an important place among the "immortals" of aviation history. Fighter, reconnaissance plane, bomber: this elegant two-engine aircraft, built entirely of wood, proved to be outstanding in practically every role. Its performance was unbeatable and it was also a deadly weapon. The key to this thoroughbred's success lay in a fortunate combination of many factors: the great care paid to its aerodynamics, the high ratio of weight to power, the pairing of an extremely effective airframe with two equally excellent engines (the Rolls-Royce Merlins). The first night fighter variant (Mk.II) went into service in the spring of 1942, and subsequently, the Mk.XII and Mk.XIII series were constructed expressly for this role.

As for the Beaufighter, this fast and powerful two-engine aircraft, designed in 1938, proved to be equally irreplaceable in a great number of roles. Tough conceived as a heavy fighter, it was used on all fronts for the entire duration of the conflict as a night fighter, fighter-bomber, torpedo plane, ground attack plane, and in anti-shipping attacks. Beginning in September 1940, the initial variant, the Mk.IF, was sent to the units of Fighter Command, and was used mainly in the role of night fighter. The aircraft of the second production version (the Mk.II) were also fighters. They were provided with two in-line Rolls-Royce Merlin engines, instead of the Bristol Hercules radials. While among the aircraft of the subsequent series, mention should be made of the Beaufighter Mk.VIFs, which were the first to be used in India and Burma.

The United States, with an immense production that excelled in practically all types of combat plane, contributed to the evolution of the heavy fighter with two aircraft in particular: the Lockheed P-38 Lightning and the Northrop P-61 Black Widow. The former, conceived in 1937, has gone down in history as one of the most effective and famous fighters of World War II. It was a particularly versatile and undoubtedly original aircraft. Moreover, it was also the first American fighter to reach more than 400 mph (644 km/h). The Lightning had a long and intensive career: interceptor, photoreconnaissance, fighter-bomber, and night fighter. Of the numerous combat missions in which it played a principal role, one of the most memorable occurred on April 18, 1943, when it intercepted and shot down the aircraft carrying Admiral Isoroku Yamamoto, the commander-in-chief of the Japanese fleet, and the brain behind the Pearl Harbor attack.

As for the Northrop P-61 Black Widow, this aircraft, designed in 1940, was not only the largest, heaviest, and most powerful fighter of the entire conflict, but also the only plane conceived expressly as a night fighter by the American aeronautical industry. In addition, it was one of the best aircraft in this category. The P-61 did not go into action until the final year of the war. Despite its bulk and weight, it was easy to handle. In addition, it was fitted with radar apparatus specially developed by the Massachusetts Institute of Technology. Its armament was particularly effective: four 20 mm cannons in the belly's pod and a similar number of 12.7 mm machine guns in a remote-controlled turret on the back of the fuselage.

1944

January 22	Anglo-American troops land at Anzio and Nettuno (Italy), but meet with heavy German resistance, blocking down their advance on Rome.
January 30	The Americans launch an offensive in the Marshall Islands.
March 2	The Japanese abandon Manila.
June 4	Allied troops enter Rome.
June 6	The Allies land in Normandy, between Cherbourg and Caen, marking the beginning of the reconquest of Europe, with the gradual surrounding of the Third Reich.
June 9	The Russians launch an offensive against Finland.
June 19-20	The Japanese air-sea forces suffer another major blow during the Battle of the Philippines Sea.
July 31	The Americans break through the German lines in Normandy (at Avranches) and begin to advance, reaching Paris on August 20.
August 23	Coup d'état in Rumania. King Michael orders the cessation of resistance against the Russians.
August 25	Liberation of Paris. The French liberation troops enter the city led by General De Gaulle.
September 4	Finland asks the Soviet Union for an armistice. Four days later, a similar decision was taken by Bulgaria, which declared war on Germany.
October 4	Greece is occupied by the Allies.
October 19	The Japanese use a desperate weapon for the first time: the kamikaze. These suicide missions, fed by great fanaticism, spread at a frightening rate.
October 24-26	Air-sea Battle of Leyte, which ended with the American landing in the Philippines.
November 2	The Germans evacuate Belgium.
November 24	First air raid on Tokyo carried out by Boeing B-29 bombers. The bases in the Mariana Islands consequently assumed a major strategic role in the course of the war against Japan.
December 30	Hungary declares war on Germany.

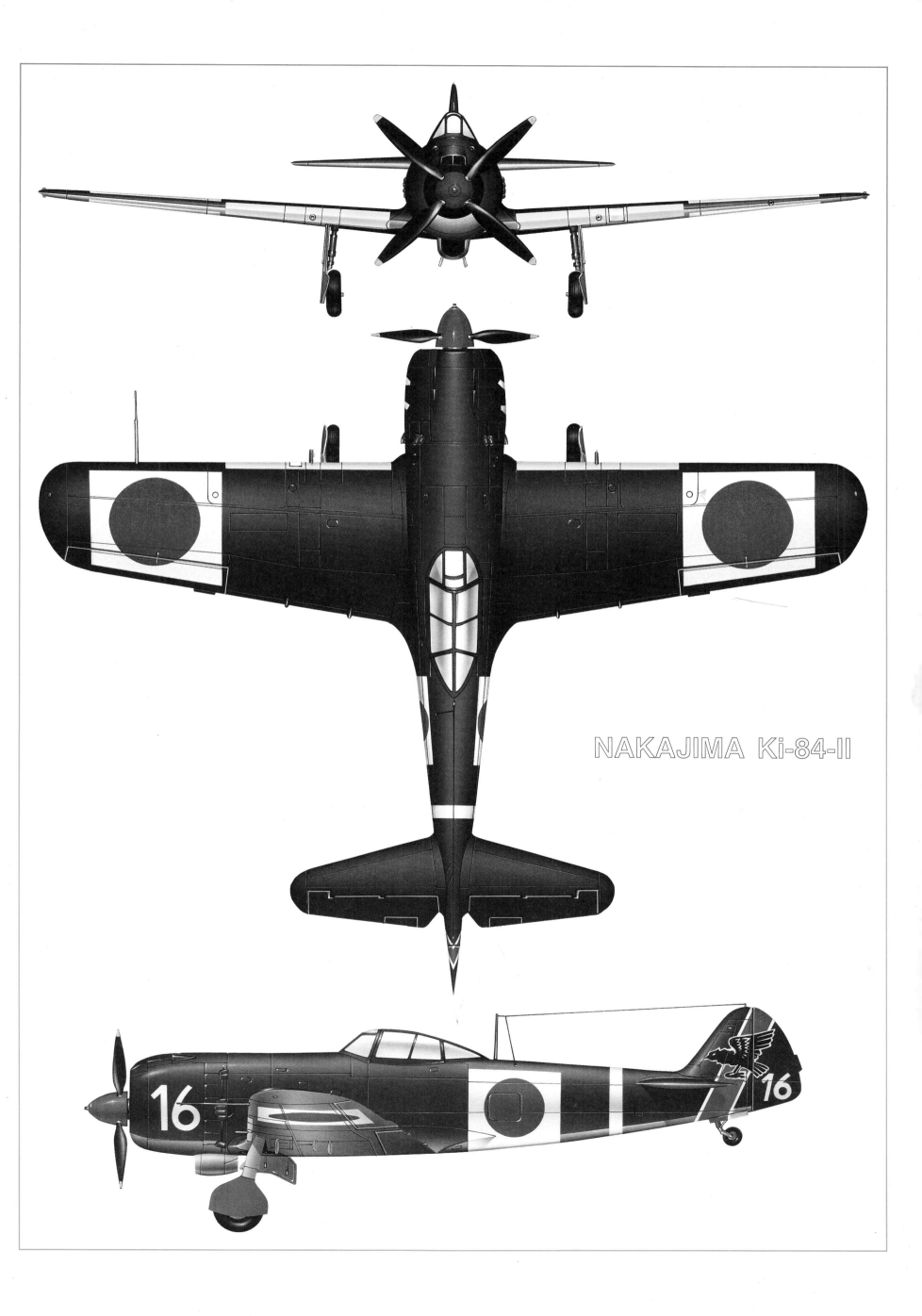

NAKAJIMA Ki-84-II

Considered the best Japanese fighter of the last two years of the war in the Pacific, the Nakajima Ki-84 Hayate (Storm) brilliantly bears witness to the great war effort carried out by the Japanese aeronautical industry in an attempt to oppose the growing American offensive. Powerful, fast, well-protected and armed, this agile interceptor proved to be completely competitive with the fiercest adversaries. A precise idea of its performance was gained after the war, in the spring of 1946, when an aircraft taken to the United States underwent a lengthy series of tests and evaluations. With a fully loaded weight of 7,505 lb (3,400 kg) the aircraft reached 426 mph (687 km/h) at an altitude of 20,050 ft (6,096 m), about 3 mph (5 km/h) faster and over 21 mph (35 km/h) more than those registered in identical conditions by a North American P-51D Mustang and a Republic P-47D Thunderbolt, respectively. These were two of the best American fighters. From March 1943 until June 1945, a total of 3,514 Nakajima Ki-84s were built, a remarkable number considering the critical conditions in which the Japanese aeronautical industry found itself: plagued and reduced to chaos by the American bombings. In the final months of the war, factories were even built underground, yet still capable of turning out 200 aircraft per month.

The project was launched at the beginning of 1942, and a year later, in April 1943, the first of the two prototypes took to the air. The aircraft was a compact all-metal low-wing monoplane with retractable landing gear, and originally powered by a 1,800 hp Nakajima Ha-45 radial engine. Its armament consisted of a pair of 12.7 mm Ho-103 machine guns installed in the engine housing and two 20 mm Ho-5 cannons installed on the wings. The initial series of tests took place without any particular problems and in the summer of 1943, the first of the initial lot of 83 pre-series aircraft were consigned to the technical units of the Imperial Army for evaluation tests. Furthermore, in October, an experimental unit was equipped with the Ki-84s, with the aim of testing them in operative conditions. The promising results led to the decision to launch series production immediately on a vast scale. The aircraft was officially designated Ki-84-la.

The model was developed in two subseries, with substantial modifications made to the armament and with a more powerful engine adopted. In the final production series, it reached 1,990 hp at takeoff. The Ki-84-lb was fitted with four 20 mm cannons, while the Ki-84-lc had two 20 mm cannons and two 30 mm Ho-105 weapons. The latter aircraft were specialized in the interception of bombers.

The increasing difficulties in supplying strategic materials led Nakajima to develop a second version (Ki-84-II) in which many components, including the rear section of the fuselage and the wing tips, were built of wood. In addition, during the last months of the war, the Tachikawa Hikoki KK built a new variant entirely of wood. Designated Ki-106, this aircraft proved to be a complete success, although the production program was initially slowed down and then suspended due to the dramatic situation of the conflict. Other projects suffered the same fate. They had been started with the aim of exploiting the already excellent characteristics of this aircraft as an interceptor. These included the high altitude Ki-84N, driven by a 2,500 hp engine, and the Ki-116, which was lighter and fitted with a 1,500 hp Mitsubishi Ha-33 radial engine.

color plate

Nakajima Ki-84-II 520th Temporary Interception Regiment for Home Island Defense, Japanese Imperial Army Air Force - Nakatsu Air Base, Japan, 1945

Aircraft:	Nakajima Ki-84-la
Nation:	Japan
Manufacturer:	Nakajima Hikoki KK
Type:	Fighter
Year:	1943
Engine:	Nakajima Ha-45, 18-cylinder radial, air-cooled, 1,900 hp
Wingspan:	36 ft 11 in (11.24 m)
Length:	32 ft 7 in (9.92 m)
Height:	11 ft 1 in (3.39 m)
Weight:	8,587 lb (3,890 kg)
Maximum speed:	390 mph (631 km/h) at 20,131 ft (6,120 m)
Ceiling:	34,540 ft (10,500 m)
Range:	1,052 miles (1,695 km)
Armament:	2 x 20 mm cannons; 2 machine guns; 1,001 lb (500 kg) of bombs
Crew:	1

A Nakajima Ki-84 that was captured, repaired and then kept in the United States.

YOKOSUKA D4Y2

The Imperial Army's Kawasaki Ki-61 and the Imperial Navy's Yokosuka D4Y Suisei were the only Japanese combat planes to be powered by a liquid-cooled in-line engine. Although they were totally different (the former was a single-seater interceptor, the latter, a two-seater dive-bomber), from many points of view these two aircraft shared a similar fate. They were both affected by continuous engine problems which prevented them from reaching their full potential. In addition, towards the end of their respective careers, they were both radically altered by the installation of the more reliable and more widely tested radial engines. However, in the case of the Yokosuka bomber, the results of this alteration were not particularly successful. From the spring of 1942 until August 1945, only 2,038 Suiseis (Comets) came off the assembly lines and their career came to an end in the final weeks of the war in the role of suicide planes.

The D4Y project was launched towards the end of 1938, and was strongly influenced by the acquisition of the license to build the German Heinkel He.118 aircraft in Japan. The characteristics of this elegant monoplane (powered by a Daimler Benz DB 601A engine) had so impressed the General Staff of the Imperial Navy that (following the destruction of the original German aircraft and the subsequent cancellation of the production program) the First Technical Arsenal of the Naval Aviation (Dai-Ichi Kaigun Koku Gijitsusho) of Yokosuka was commissioned to design a carrier-based dive-bomber directly based on the Heinkel He.118 prototype. The specifications included a maximum speed of 322 mph (518 km/h) and a cruising speed of 265 mph (426 km/h), a range of 800 nautical miles (1,482 km) with a 550 lb (250 kg) bomb load and 1,380 miles (2,223 km) without a bomb load. In addition, the ability to operate from smaller aircraft carriers was also required. Furthermore, the engine chosen was the Daimler Benz DB 601A, produced on license by Aichi.

However, due to delays in the construction of the German engine, the first D4Y1 was provided with a 960 hp DB 600, imported directly from Germany. Despite its inferior power, the prototype (completed in November 1940, and flown for the first time the following month) made an excellent impression thanks to its remarkable characteristics and its superior technical and aerodynamic qualities. Nevertheless, as flight tests proceeded, the aircraft developed serious structural problems when used as a dive-bomber, and the search for a solution proved to be slow. It was not until March 1943, that the Suisei was accepted by the Navy in this specific role. In the meantime, production had been launched and the first production series aircraft were used for reconnaissance. At the same time, its experiences as an attack plane were not successful. Intended to replace the by then obsolete Aichi D3A2s, the D4Y1s proved to be indefensible and, more importantly, plagued by unreliable engines. Their vulnerability was fully revealed in the summer of 1944, during the battles to prevent the Americans from landing in the Mariana Islands.

Not even the appearance in October 1944, of the subsequent variant (the D4Y2, with a more powerful engine and heavier defensive armament) changed the situation. Following the construction of 660 D4Y1s and 326 D4Y2s, production continued with 536 D4Y3s (in which a 1,560 hp Mitsubishi Kinsei 62 radial engine was adopted) and with 296 D4Y4s, specialized in suicide attacks. In fact, it was in one of these aircraft that, on August 15, 1945, Admiral Ugaki carried out the last kamikaze attack of the war, against the American fleet at Okinawa. At the time of the Japanese surrender, the D4Y5, final bomber's version, was at an advanced stage of development. It was better protected and powered by a 1,670 hp Nakajima Homare 12 radial engine.

---

color plate

Yokosuka D4Y2 2nd Section of Yokosuka Kokutai Japanese Imperial Navy Air Force - Japan 1945

Aircraft:	Yokosuka D4Y1
Nation:	Japan
Manufacturer:	Aichi Kokuki KK
Type:	Bomber
Year:	1943
Engine:	Aichi AE1A Atsuta, 12-cylinder V, liquid-cooled, 1,200 hp
Wingspan:	37 ft 9 in (11.50 m)
Length:	33 ft 7 in (10.22 m)
Height:	12 ft 1 in (3.68 m)
Weight:	9,381 lb (4,250 kg)
Maximum speed:	342 mph (552 km/h) at 15,625 ft (4,750 m)
Ceiling:	32,565 ft (9,900 m)
Range:	978 miles (1,575 km)
Armament:	3 x machine guns; 684 lb (310 kg) of bombs
Crew:	2

A Yokosuka D4Y2 taking-off from an airport in the South.

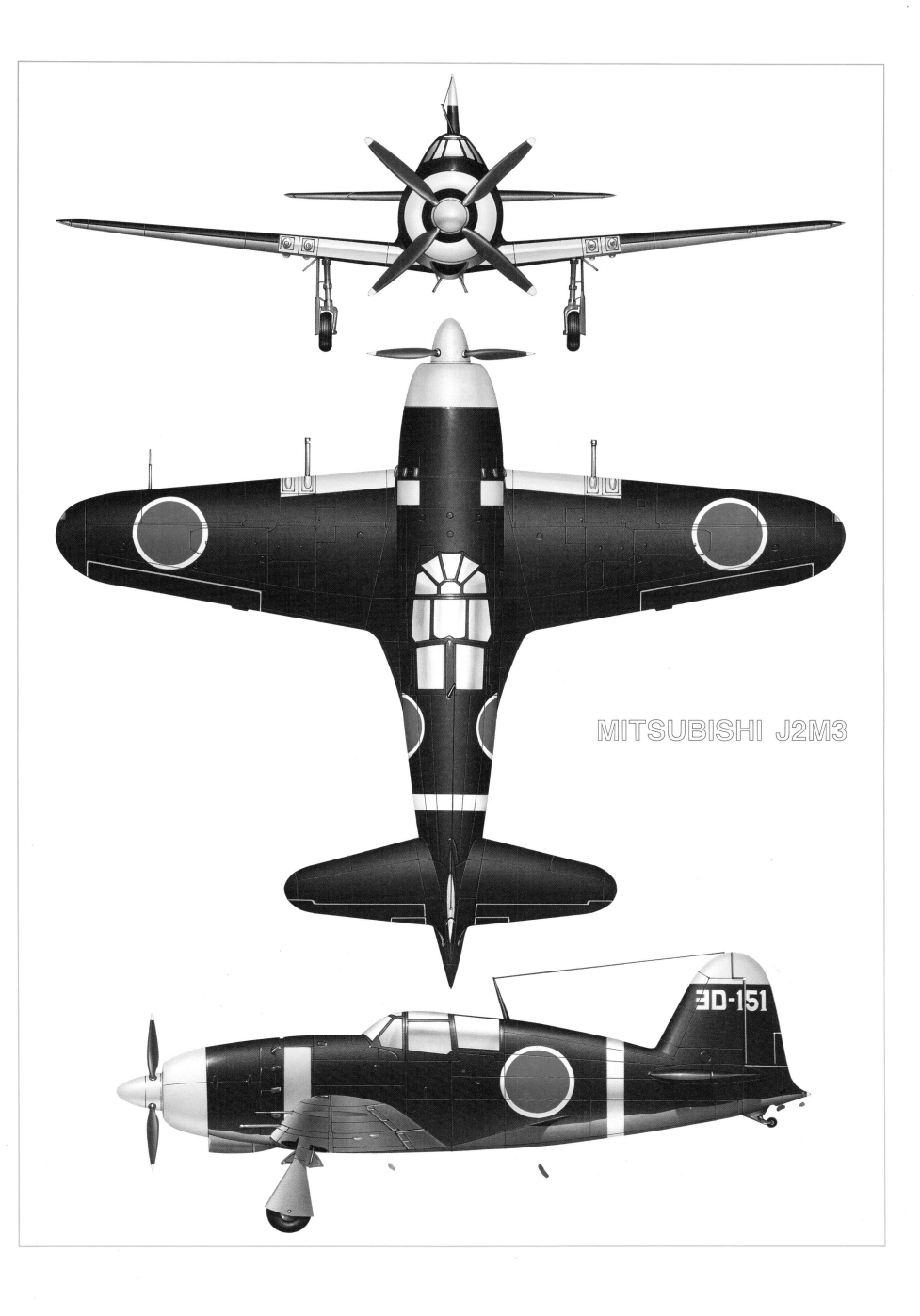

MITSUBISHI J2M3

Although it was designed in October 1938, almost five years passed before the Mitsubishi J2M Raiden (Lightning) was used in combat. In fact, the preparation of this interceptor took an extremely long time, due above all to numerous technical problems connected with the functioning of the engines, which were never entirely resolved. Only 476, including the various prototypes, came off the assembly lines and most of these were used to defend Japan during the last months of the war.

The Imperial Navy had issued a request for a land-based interceptor some months after the program for the Mitsubishi A6M Reisen (the famous Zero) had been launched, and this coincidental timing was the primary cause for the delays. In fact, since all of Mitsubishi's technical staff was occupied with the development of the new fighter, eleven months were to pass before the exact specifications were defined. The requests included a maximum speed of 372 mph (600 km/h) at 19,736 ft (6,000 m), the ability to climb to the same altitude in less than five and a half minutes, and the ability to operate at combat speed for 45 minutes. These characteristics, which for the first time called for qualities of horizontal speed and ascent (in an interceptor), rather than those concerning range and maneuverability, indicated a change in mentality in the general staff of the navy, as well as great foresight.

However, this foresight was not compensated by practical results. The first of three prototypes took to the air on March 20, 1942, and a whole series of problems immediately emerged. A further eight months were necessary to solve them. The initial problems concerned the retracting mechanism of the main landing gear as well as that which regulated the pitch of the propeller. Later on, problems occurred with the engine, a large 1,430 hp Kasei 13 radial, which drove the propeller by means of a transmission shaft. A decision to pull back the propeller consequently improved the aerodynamics of the aircraft. In addition, the Imperial Navy's pilots complained of highly limited visibility through the windscreen.

It was thus necessary to carry out many modifications and as a result, even the original engine was replaced by the more powerful Kasei 23, which generated 1,800 hp at takeoff. However this change was the cause of fresh problems. The engine, that possessed a water and gas injection system to increase its power in the case of an emergency, was the first of its kind to be developed by the Japanese aeronautical industry, and it proved to be the source of complex tuning problems. In addition,

Two Mitsubishi Raidens tested in flight by the Allies following their capture.

dangerous vibrations within the engine at certain speeds also had to be eliminated.

The fighter went into production in December 1942, with the designation J2M2, but after only a few months the assembly lines came to a halt. Soon after, the cause of two inexplicable accidents was discovered: the mistaken position of the tail wheel's retracting mechanism which, set in motion immediately after takeoff, blocked the controls in a diving position. It was not until December 1943, that the Raiden was ready and by that time a new version (J2M3) with heavier armament was already prepared. Production completed 155 J2M2s and 281 J2M3s, plus 34 J2M5s, fitted with a Kasei 26 engine generating 1,820 hp at takeoff. However, the fighter retained its initial faults, even in the new versions. Nevertheless, the Raiden remained active right up till the end of the conflict, and scored several successes in the struggle against the enemy bombers.

---

color plate

Mitsubishi J2M3 1st Hilotai 302nd Kokutai Imperial Japanese Navy Air Force - Atsugi Airfield, Tokyo 1944-1945

A Mitsubishi J2M3 during takeoff.

Aircraft:	Mitsubishi J2M3
Nation:	Japan
Manufacturer:	Mitsubishi Jukogyo KK
Type:	Fighter
Year:	1943
Engine:	Mitsubishi MK4R-A Kasei 23, 14-cylinder radial, air-cooled, 1,800 hp
Wingspan:	35 ft 7 in (10.82 m)
Length:	32 ft 8 in (9.95 m)
Height:	12 ft 11 in (3.95 m)
Weight:	7,560 lb (3,435 kg)
Maximum speed:	369 mph (595 km/h) at 19,407 ft (5,900 m)
Ceiling:	38,486 ft (11,700 m)
Range:	1,179 miles (1,900 km)
Armament:	4 x 20 mm cannons; 264 lb (120 kg) of bombs
Crew:	1

JAPAN

Just as Pearl Harbor had marked the beginning of the war in the Pacific, and Midway had characterized its turning point, the third phase, which was to lead to the definitive defeat of Japan, started in the summer of 1944. In the process of reconquering the territories occupied by the Japanese forces, the prelude to the final attack on the Empire of the Rising Sun, the possession of the Mariana archipelago by the Americans had a strategic value that went well beyond the actual physical dimensions of these small islands lost in the immensity of the Pacific.

In fact, with the availability of this advanced base, a veritable thorn in the side of Japan's military plans, the Allies were able for the first time to operate freely within the range of action of the brand new Boeing B-29 heavy bombers. It was from the bases in the Mariana Islands that the threatening and devastating bombing raids on Japan were launched. These were to culminate in August 1945, with the dropping of the two atomic bombs on Hiroshima and Nagasaki.

Thus, once again, the aircraft proved to be the unquestionable protagonist in determining the outcome of the conflict. Until then, this new combat phase had been carried out from airports in China. The first bombing mission on Japan had been carried out on June 15, 1944, by 68 B-29s that had taken off from Chengtu, releasing their deadly bomb load on the steel plants of Kyushu. This was the first strategic bombing raid to which the Empire of the Rising Sun had been subjected, coming two years after the purely symbolic one carried out by Doolittle's B-25s on April 18, 1942. It also marked the beginning of a deadly offensive which was to bring the enemy to its knees, causing chaos in its industrial network and weakening the psychological resistance of the population.

The first raid on Tokyo, carried out from the bases on the Mariana Islands, took place on November 24, 1944. Until August 6, 1945, the Boeing B-29s continued these specialized raids with incendiary bombs, initially by day, and then by night at low altitude.

However, apart from these purely military effects, the Japanese defeat in the Mariana Islands also had much more serious consequences on a political level. On July 18, Japan's prime minister, General Hideki Tojo, resigned after a similar gesture had been made by Admiral Shimada, minister for the Navy. These resignations gave rise to a final period of uncertainty and disorientation in Japan's government.

Nevertheless, on a military level, Japan's defense continued to be tenacious in the slow withdrawal (under pressure by the American offensive) from the territories conquered two years earlier. Moreover, in order to oppose the by now unbeatable superiority of the enemy in terms both of men and aircraft, Japan increased still further its already high production rate.

The growing Allied pressure and the beginning of bombings on Japanese territory did not hamper the war effort. On the contrary, in the aeronautical field, qualitative and quantitative progress was achieved at an extremely high level as far as the production of aircraft and engines was concerned. However, it was practically impossible for the air forces of the Imperial Army and Imperial Navy to replace the slow hemorrhage of skilled and trained veterans with pilots and crews who were equally well prepared.

The aeronautical production figures for the last years of the war are the clearest indication of how great Japan's industrial potential was. In 1943, a total of 16,693 aircraft were built (7,147 fighters, and 4,189 bombers) as well as 28,541 engines and 31,703 propellers. In 1944, the number of aircraft increased to 28,180 of all types (13,811 fighters and 5,100 bombers), while production of engines and propellers reached 46,526 and 54,452, respectively. It should be remembered that in 1938, the Japanese aeronautical industry had produced 3,201 aircraft of all types, this figure increasing to 4,467 in 1939, and to 4,768 in 1940. In addition, in 1941, 5,080 aircraft of all types had come off the assembly lines (including 1,080 fighters and 1,461 bombers), and in the same year, the production of propellers and engines had totaled 12,621 and 12,151, respectively. In 1942, aeronautical production had almost doubled with 8,861 aircraft being completed, including 2,935 fighters and 2,433 bombers, while 16,999 engines and 22,362 propellers were built.

Chronology

1943

February. The first Kawasaki Ki-61-I Hiens reach the units. This was the only fighter with an in-line liquid-cooled engine to be built by the Japanese during the conflict. In all, 2,753 were built in several versions, and although they were generally effective, they were always to be plagued by problems regarding the tuning of the power plants.

April 18. Death of Admiral Isoroku Yamamoto, the artificer of Pearl Harbor and the Empire of the Rising Sun's main strategist. His aircraft, a two-engine Mitsubishi G4M Betty, was shot down by a formation of American Lockheed P-38 Lightning fighters above Bougainville, following a daring interception.

December 31. The prototype of the Kawanishi N1K2-J Shiden takes to the air for the first time. A new, highly modified version of the N1K1-J fighter, the aircraft was accepted immediately by the Imperial Navy as a fighter and standard land fighter-bomber. A vast production program was launched in June 1944, with all of the major Japanese aeronautical manufacturers taking part. However, this objective was never achieved, due to the Japan's critical situation. In the country, devastated by the incessant bombing raids Carried out by the Americans, just 423 N1K2-Js came off the assembly lines before the end of the war.

1944

April. The Nakajima Ki-84 Hayate, considered the best Japanese fighter of the last years of the war, makes its debut in combat. Fast, powerful, well-protected and well-armed, this agile interceptor proved to be fully competitive with the most efficient enemy aircraft. Up till June 1945, 3,514 Nakajima Ki-84s were built, a considerable number in view of the critical conditions of the Japanese industrial network that was plagued and reduced to chaos by the bombing raids.

June 15. Japan is subjected to the first raid carried out by American B-29s, which, in this phase of the war, operated from bases in China. These raids acquired increasing weight and intensity until the final day of the conflict.

October 13. The prototype of the Mitsubishi A7M2 takes to the air. Only nine prototypes and one production series aircraft were completed before the war ended.

October 25. Japan launches the final, desperate missions against the Allied forces: the kamikaze suicide attacks. These first occurred in the Battle of Leyte Gulf, in which Mitsubishi A6M5 fighters prepared for this task were employed. In these missions without return, an escort aircraft carrier, the *St Lo*, was sunk.

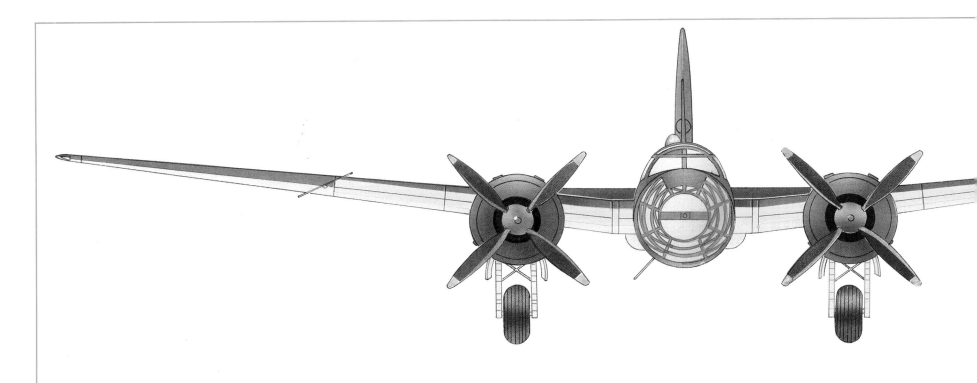

MITSUBISHI Ki-67

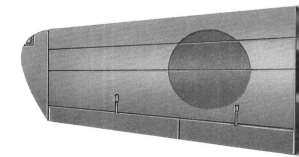

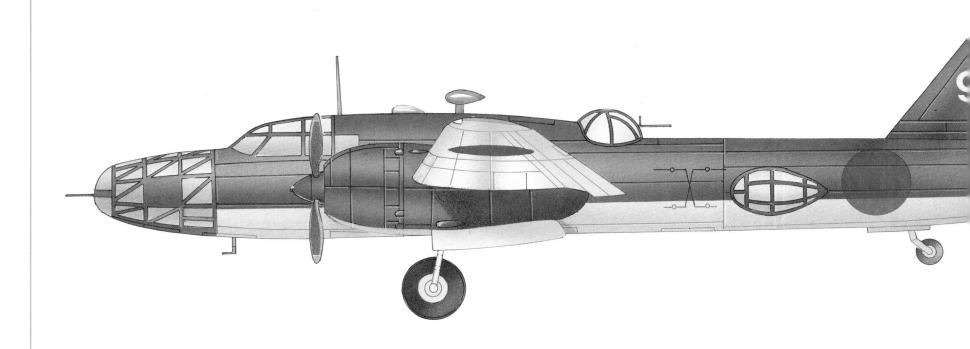

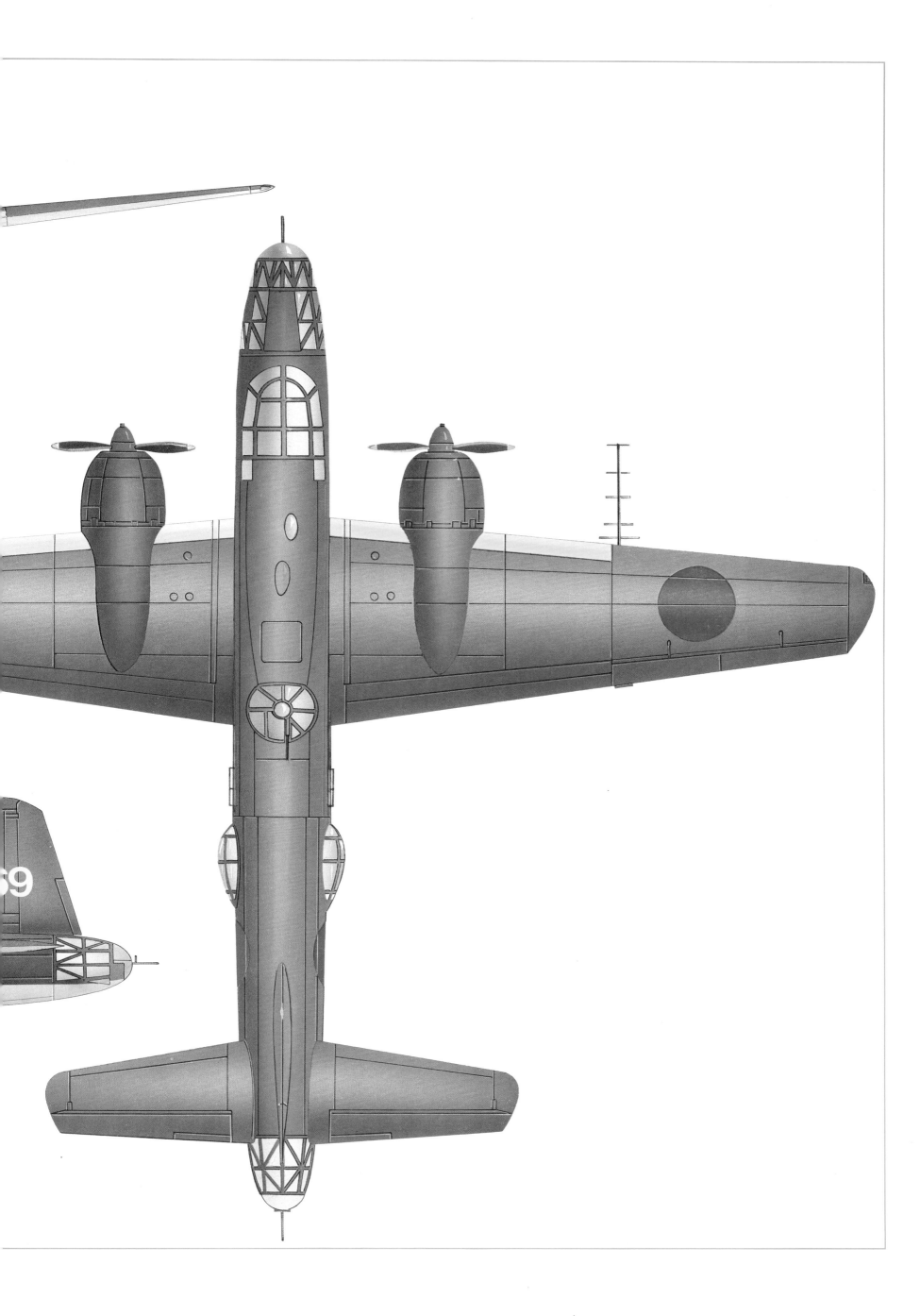

Considered the best Japanese bomber of the war in the Pacific, the Mitsubishi Ki-67 Hiryu (Flying Dragon) was also the last aircraft in this category to be used in any number by the Imperial Army. Fast, agile, and well-armed, this elegant two-engine aircraft was officially classified as a heavy bomber, although in practice, according to the standards of the Allies, it could have been included in the category of medium bombers (such as the B-25 or the B-26). Nevertheless, the Ki-67 proved to be an outstanding combat plane, and its only limitations were that it arrived too late on the scene of the conflict, and was employed in too small a number. The startling potential of these bombers was revealed during the desperate Japanese counteroffensive on Iwo Jima and the Mariana Islands, and during the American landings at Okinawa. In all, 698 came off the assembly lines and production was given maximum priority right until the last day of the war.

The specifications for a successor to the Nakajima Ki-49 Donryu were defined in February 1941, when Mitsubishi was asked to build three prototypes of a new bomber with modern characteristics. The specifications called for a maximum speed of 341 mph (550 km/h), a bomb load of 1,766 lb (800 kg), and an operative ceiling between 13,157 ft (4,000 m) and 23,026 ft (7,000 m). Moreover, the defensive armament was to consist of five machine guns, while the crew was to range from a standard of 6-8 members, to a maximum of 10 in certain situations. Mitsubishi's technicians developed the project bearing in mind easy assembly and maintenance, paying very close attention to its protection, both of the crew and the fuel tanks. The aircraft took on the form of a slender all-metal middle-wing two-engine plane with retractable landing gear. It was powered by a pair of 1,900 hp Ha-104 radial engines that drove four-bladed metal variable-pitch propellers. The three prototypes were completed respectively in December 1942, and February and March of the following year. The first of them took to the air on December 27, 1942. The initial series of tests did not bring to light any particular defects; in fact, they fully confirmed the excellent characteristics of the project. So much so that it was also decided to employ the aircraft in the role of torpedo plane.

Series production was launched on December 3, 1943, under the official designation of Ki-67-I, and starting with the 160th, the aircraft were also fitted with an external support for a torpedo.

The Hiryu made its debut in an anti-shipping attack, in October 1944, during the violent air-sea battles off Formosa. From then onward, the two-engined Mitsubishis were employed both by the army and the navy, in all the principal theaters of operations.

In the course of production very few modifications were made to original, although several experimental variants were designed during the last year of the war. Of these, the only one that went into production (22 built in all) was the Ki-67 that was transformed into a heavy fighter. Designated Ki-109, the aircraft was characterized by the installation of a 75 mm cannon in the nose. This weapon, provided with 15 bullets, was meant for use against the B-29s that flew at great altitude. The tests produced good results; however in practice the effectiveness of this type of operation was cancelled due to the low altitude night bombing raids carried out by the American bombers.

color plate

Mitsubishi Ki-67 98th Bomber Sentai 3rd Chutai Japanese Imperial Air Force - Okinawa, 1945

Aircraft:	Mitsubishi Ki-67-I
Nation:	Japan
Manufacturer:	Mitsubishi Jukogyo KK
Type:	Bomber
Year:	1944
Engine:	2 Mitsubishi Ha-104, 14-cylinder radial, air-cooled, 1,900 hp each
Wingspan:	74 ft 0 in (22.50 m)
Length:	61 ft 6 in (18.70 m)
Height:	25 ft 3 in (7.70 m)
Weight:	30,386 lb (13,765 kg)
Maximum speed:	333 mph (537 km/h) at 20,032 ft (6,090 m)
Ceiling:	31,151 ft (9,470 m)
Range:	2,360 miles (3,800 km)
Armament:	1 x 20 mm cannon; 4 machine guns; 1,766 lb (800 kg) of bombs
Crew:	6-8

A Mitsubishi Ki-67 Hiryu bearing American insignia during tests carried out after its capture.

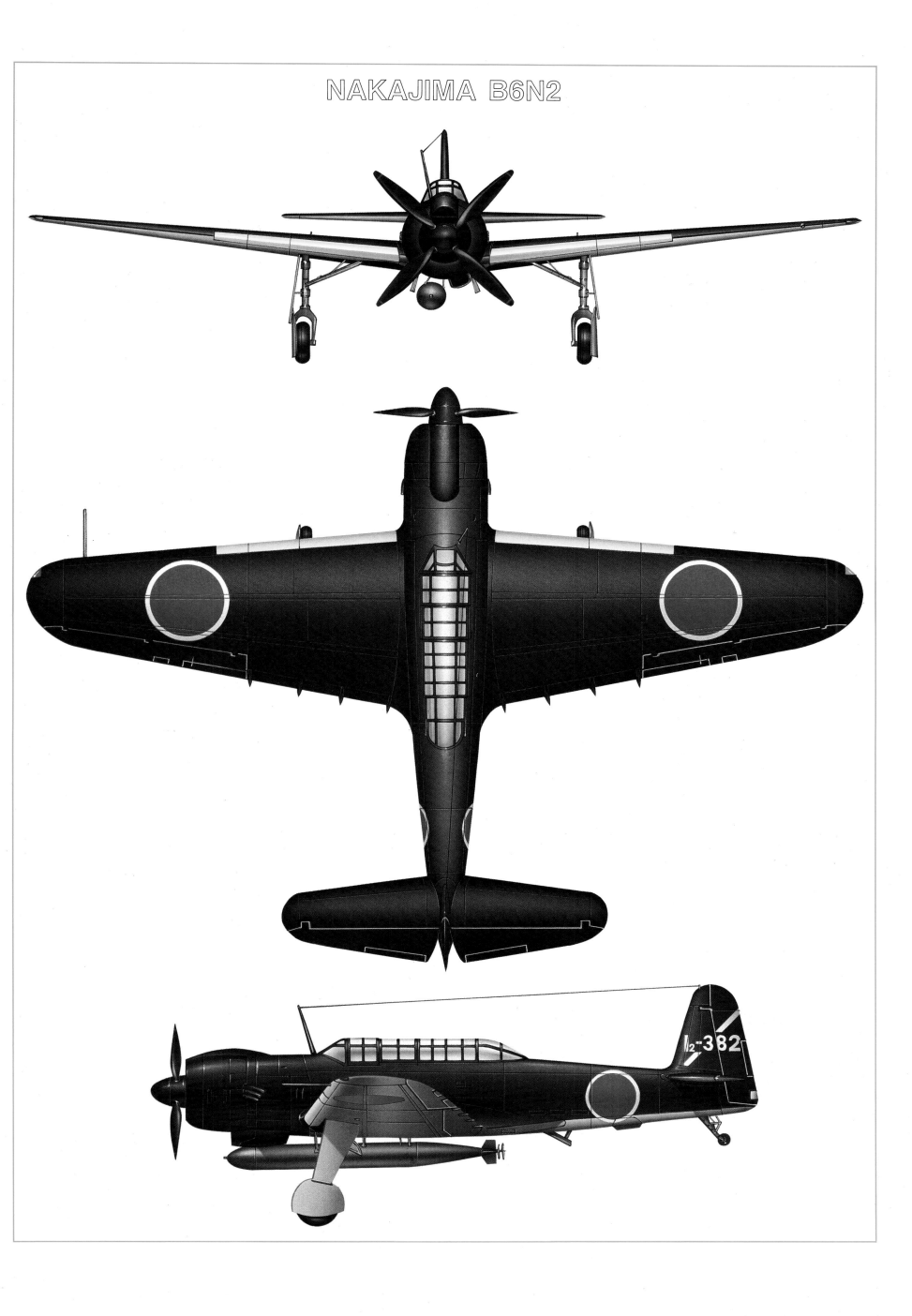

NAKAJIMA B6N2

Intended to replace the Nakajima B5N in the role of carrier-based torpedo plane, the B6N Tenzan (Mountain of the Sky) was designed toward the end of 1939, although it went into service much later, after more than two years of evaluations. In all, 1,268 were built, in two principal variants. Their careers were particularly intensive during the last two years of the war.

The specifications issued by the navy called for very modern characteristics: a maximum speed of 288 mph (463 km/h), a cruising speed of 230 mph (370 km/h) and a range of 1,000 nautical miles (1,853 km) with a 1,766 lb (800 kg) torpedo and of 1,800 nautical miles (3,335 km) without a bomb load. The project was carried out under the direction of Kenichi Matsamura, who basically took his inspiration from the airframe of the plane's direct predecessor. The new torpedo plane retained the general configuration of the B5N; however, the structure of the tail planes was substantially modified. Despite the fact that the navy insisted that the aircraft be provided with a Mitsubishi Kasei radial engine, the designer chose the new 1,870 hp Nakajima Mamoru engine, characterized by relatively low specific consumption. The first of the two prototypes was completed in the early months of 1941, and was ready for its first tests in the spring.

However, evaluations brought to light a number of problems, the most serious of which concerned the aircraft's directional stability. Subsequently, the preparation phase of the aircraft was further delayed by difficulties in the tuning of the engine and the need to reinforce the landing gear and arrester hook. This particular weakness had emerged during the final tests carried out toward the end of 1942, on board the aircraft carriers *Ryuho* and *Zuikaku*.

Production finally got under way in February 1943, although further problems emerged. After 135 of the initial B6N1 version had been completed, Nakajima received an order to suspend production of the Mamoru engine and to install the more reliable Mitsubishi Kasei 25 on the Tenzan. Thus, the second and major variant of the aircraft (the B6N2) was prepared and it began to come off the assembly lines in June. In all, up till August 1945, 1,133 aircraft were completed in this version.

In combat, the Tenzan behaved satisfactorily, although it was never an outstanding aircraft. Its employment on board ship was limited to the larger aircraft carriers due to its high landing speed and heavy wing load.

Very few modifications were introduced in the course of production. The aircraft of the final series (designated B6N2a) had

A Nakajima B6N2 with folded wings.

heavier armament (a 13 mm machine gun, instead of the 7.7 mm weapon on the aircraft's back). Two of this subseries served as prototypes for a new variant (the B6N3) which was fitted with a Mitsubishi MK4T-C Kasei 25c engine generating 1,850 hp at takeoff, and with a reinforced landing gear, suitable also for operations on land and semi-prepared runways. However, this final version never went into production.

color plate
Nakajima B6N2 aircraft-carrier *Zuikaku*, Japanese Imperial Navy Air Force - Pacific area, 1944

Aircraft:	Nakajima B6N2
Nation:	Japan
Manufacturer:	Nakajima Hikoki KK
Type:	Torpedo plane
Year:	1943
Engine:	Mitsubishi MK4T Kasei 25, 14-cylinder radial, air-cooled, 1,850 hp
Wingspan:	49 ft 0 in (14.90 m)
Length:	35 ft 9 in (10.87 m)
Height:	12 ft 6 in (3.80 m)
Weight:	12,472 lb (5,650 kg)
Maximum speed:	298 mph (481 km/h) at 16,118 ft (4,900 m)
Ceiling:	29,736 ft (9,040 m)
Range:	1,890 miles (3,045 km)
Armament:	2 machine guns; 1,766 lb (800 kg) of bombs
Crew:	3

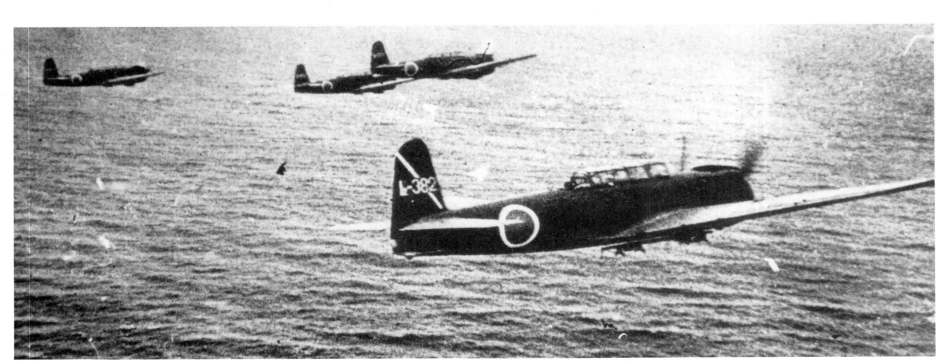
A formation of Nakajima Tenzan in flight at low altitude over the ocean.

GRUMMAN F6F-5

During 1943, superiority in the air, firmly in the hands of the Japanese since Pearl Harbor, began to weigh decisively in favor of the Americans. The Grumman F6F Hellcat, together with the Vought F4U Corsair, was the aircraft that most contributed to this decisive redressing of the balance. Fast, powerful, well-armed and protected, this outstanding combat plane represented the high point of the American carrier-based aviation in the last two years of the war. The importance of the Hellcat in the conflict in the Pacific is clearly shown by the production figures and by those of its combat activity. In all, 12,275 came off the assembly lines. The aircraft began its career on August 31, 1943. It succeeded in shooting down a remarkable number of aircraft. Out of a total of 6,477 enemy planes destroyed by the carrier-based pilots, no fewer than 4,947 fell under the Hellcats' fire. This figure increases to 5,156 if one adds the victories scored by the F6Fs based on land and those serving in the U.S. Marine Corps.

The project was developed by Grumman in order to build a successor to the F4F Wildcat, and the contract for the construction of two prototypes was signed on June 30, 1941. The program went forward very quickly and the first experimental version (designated XF6F-1) took to the air a year later on June 26, 1942. The aircraft was a large all-metal low-wing monoplane with retractable landing gear and arrester hook. It was fitted with a 1,700 hp Wright R-2600-10 engine and it was joined a month later, by the second prototype, in which the more powerful Pratt & Whitney R-2800-10 engine had been installed. From this aircraft, designated XF6F-3, the first series version was derived. This began to leave the assembly lines at the beginning of October, on the basis of the first, massive orders placed by the U.S. Navy back

in May. The installation of a more powerful engine proved decisive for the future success of the Hellcat, in that it allowed it to absorb the notable weight increase suffered in the course of production without a substantial reduction in performance. Their first assignments took place on January 16, 1943, when they were delivered to the aircraft carrier *Essex*, and on August 31, to the aircraft carriers *Essex*, *Yorktown* and *Independence*. The F6F-3s had their baptism of fire during an attack on the island of Marcus.

In the meantime, production was going ahead at a substantial pace: during 1943, 2,545 F6F-3s were delivered, 252 of which went to the British Fleet Air Arm that christened them Hellcat Mk.I and put them into service in July. In all, 4,403 of the first version left the assembly lines and of these, 205 were equipped as night fighters and designated F6F-3E and F6F-3N.

On April 4, 1944, the first F6F-5 variant of the Hellcat took to the air. This was the major production variant, with 7,870 being built, of which 932 were given to the British Navy. It differed from the previous version above all in its engine (a Pratt & Whitney R-2800-10W with water injection to increase power in the case of emergency) and in its heavier armament, which eventually included a maximum bomb load of 2,002 lb (907 kg). A series of night fighters (F6F-5N) were derived from this version too, with 1,434 being built in all. Production ceased on November 16, 1945.

color plate
Grumman F6F-5 VF-17 aircraft carrier *Hornet* U.S. Navy Air Force - Pacific area 1945

Aircraft:	Grumman F6F-3
Nation:	USA
Manufacturer:	Grumman Aircraft Engineering Corp.
Type:	Fighter
Year:	1943
Engine:	Pratt & Whitney R-2800-10 Double Wasp, 18-cylinder radial, air-cooled, 2,000 hp
Wingspan:	42 ft 11 in (13.05 m)
Length:	33 ft 10 in (10.31 m)
Height:	12 ft 7 in (3.9 m)
Weight:	15,507 lb (7,025 kg)
Maximum speed:	375 mph (605 km/h) at 20,052 ft (6,096 m)
Ceiling:	37,398 ft (11,369 m)
Range:	1,089 miles (1,754 km)
Armament:	6 machine guns
Crew:	1

An F6F-3 equipped with a radar on its wings and used as a night fighter.

A F6F-5 bearing post-war insignia.

ALLIED IDENTIFICATION CODE FOR JAPANESE AIRCRAFT

The designation system for the aircraft used in Japan by the army and the navy was particularly complex, and certainly did not facilitate identification on the part of the adversary. Thus, in order to simplify and more easily recognize the Empire of the Rising Sun's aircraft, the Allies invented a special code, that basically assigned a name to every Japanese aircraft in service.

In principal, male names were given to fighters and reconnaissance seaplanes; female names were given to bombers, reconnaissance planes, and seaplanes; names of trees were given to trainers; names of birds to gliders. However, in practice, this identification code was not particularly rigid, and there were numerous exceptions. This was due above all to the inevitable confusion of the combat reports.

Here is a list of code names assigned by the Allies to the main types of Japanese aircraft that were in service during World War II.

ABDUL	Nakajima Ki-27 (duplication for NATE)
ALF	Kawanishi E7K
ANN	Mitsubishi Ki-30
BABS	Mitsubishi Ki-15 / Mitsubishi C5M
BAKA	Yokosuka MXY7 Ohka
BETTY	Mitsubishi G4M1/G4M3
CEDAR	Tachikawa Ki-17
CHERRY	Yokosuka H5Y
CLAUDE	Mitsubishi A5M
CYPRESS	Kyushu K9W / Kokusai Ki-86
DAVE	Nakajima E8N
DICK	Seversky A8V1
DINAH	Mitsubishi Ki-46
DOT	Yokosuka D4Y Suisei (Duplication for JUDY)
EMILY	Kawanishi H8K
EVA (EVE)	Mitsubishi Ohtori
FRANCES	Yokosuka P1Y Ginga / Yokosuka P1Y1-S Byakko / Yokosuka P1Y2-S Kyokko
FRANK	Nakajima Ki-84 Hayate
GANDER	Kokusai Ku-8 (formerly GOOSE)
GEORGE	Kawanishi N1K1-J/N1K5-J Shiden and Shiden Kai
GLEN	Yokosuka E14Y
GOOSE	Kokusai Ku-8 (later GANDER)
GRACE	Aichi B7A Ryusei
GWEN	Mitsubishi Ki-21-IIb (later SALLY III)
HAMP	Mitsubishi A6M3 (this aircraft was first coded HAP, then HAMP, and finally ZEKE 32)
HELEN	Nakajima Ki-49 Donryu
HICKORY	Tachikawa Ki-54
IDA	Tachikawa Ki-36 / Tachikawa Ki-55
IRVING	Nakajima J1N1-C and -R / Nakajima J1N1-S Gekko
JACK	Mitsubishi J2M Raiden
JAKE	Aichi E13A
JANE	Mitsubishi Ki-21 (later changed to SALLY)
JEAN	Yokosuka B4Y
JILL	Nakajima B6N Tenzan
JIM	Nakajima Ki-43 Hayabusa (duplication for OSCAR)
JUDY	Yokosuka D4Y1-C/D4Y2-Ca / Yokosuka D4Y Suisei
KATE	Nakajima B5N

KATE 61	Mitsubishi B5M (formerly MABEL)
LAURA	Aichi E11A
LILY	Kawasaki Ki-48
LIZ	Nakajima G5N Shinzan
LORNA	Kyushu Q1W
LOISE/LOUISE	Mitsubishi Ki-2
MABEL	Mitsubishi B5M (later KATE 61)
MARY	Kawasaki Ki-32
MAVIS	Kawanishi H6K
MYRT	Nakajima C6N Saiun
NATE	Nakajima Ki-27
NELL	Mitsubishi G3M / Yokosuka L3Y
NICK	Kawasaki Ki-45 KAI Toryu
NORM	Kawanishi E15K Shiun
OAK	Kyushu K10W
OSCAR	Nakajima Ki-43 Hayabusa
PAT	Tachikawa Ki-74
PAUL	Aichi E16A Zuiun
PEGGY	Mitsubishi Ki-67 Hiryu
PERRY	Kawasaki Ki-10
PETE	Mitsubishi F1M
PINE	Mitsubishi K3M
RANDY	Kawasaki Ki-102b
REX	Kawanishi N1K Kyofu
RITA	Nakajima G8N Renzan
RUFE	Nakajima A6M2-N
SALLY	Mitsubishi Ki-21 (formerly JANE)
SAM	Mitsubishi A7M Reppu
SANDY	Mitsubishi A5M (duplication for CLAUDE)
SONIA	Mitsubishi Ki-51
SPRUCE	Tachikawa Ki-9
STELLA	Kokusai Ki-76
SUSIE	Aichi D1A1 / Aichi D1A2
THALIA	Kawasaki Ki-56
THERESA	Kokusai Ki-59
THORA	Nakajima Ki-34 / Nakajima L1N
TINA	Mitsubishi Ki-33
TOJO	Nakajima Ki-44 Shoki
TONY	Kawasaki Ki-61 Hien
TOPSY	Mitsubishi Ki-57 / Mitsubishi L4M
VAL	Aichi D3A
WILLOW	Yokosuka K5Y
ZEKE	Mitsubishi A6M

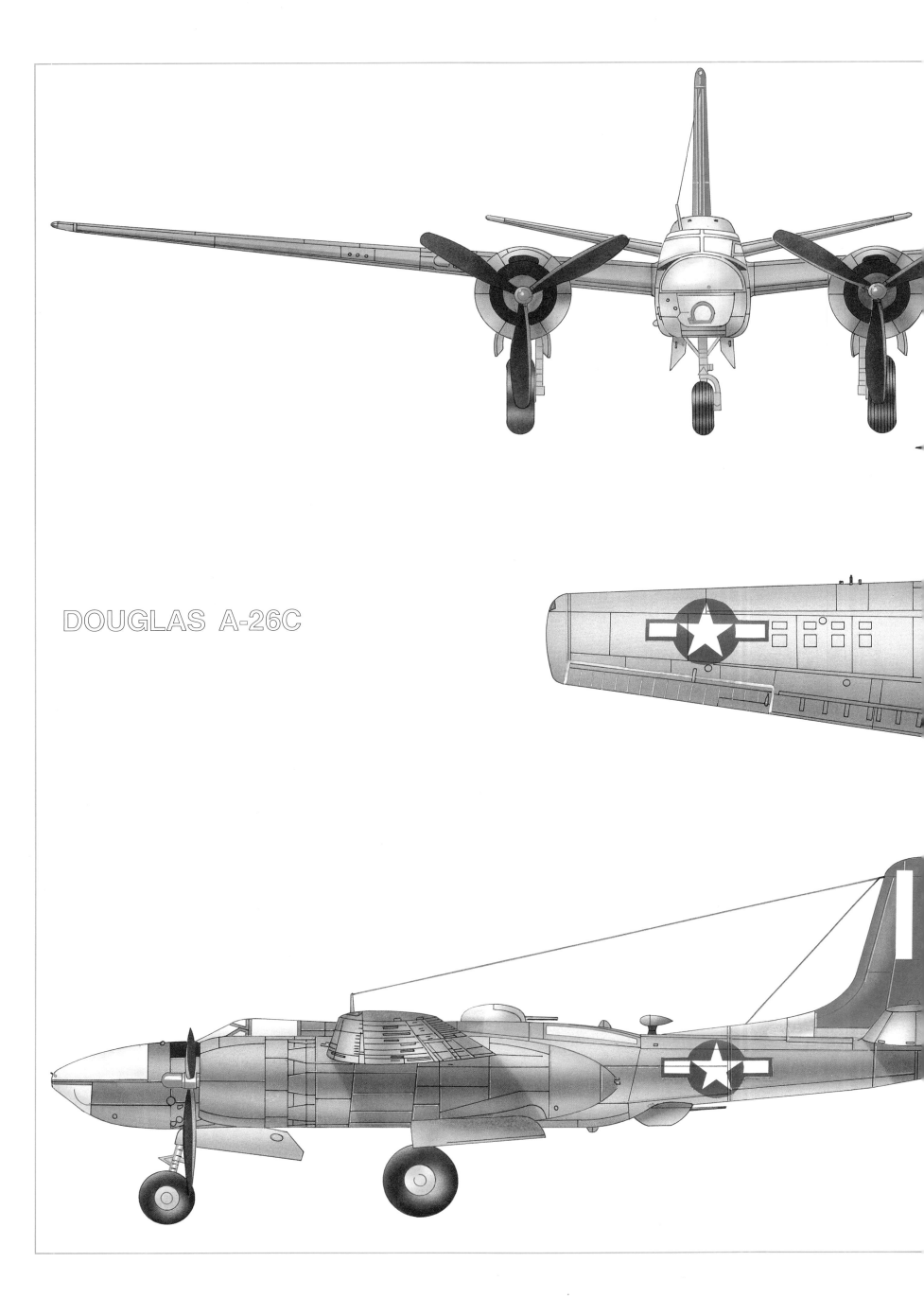

DOUGLAS A-26C

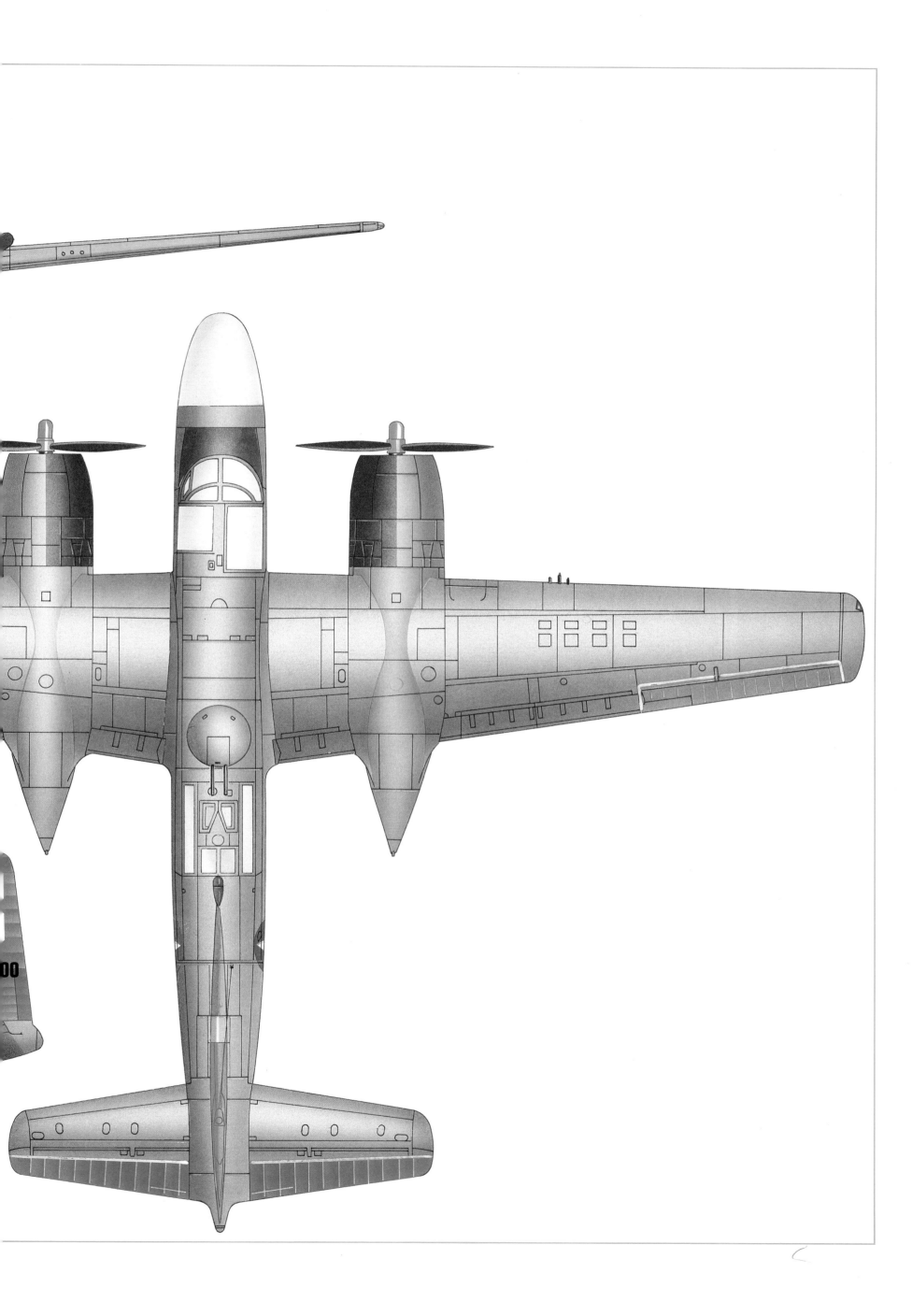

Considered the best ground attack plane and tactical bomber sent into combat by the American aviation, the Douglas A-26 Invader represented the high point in the development of a family of high performance two-engined light aircraft that Douglas had started to build back in 1936, with the DB-7 and the later Boston-Havocs. 2,446 Invaders were built in two main versions. The end of the war led to the cancellation of a further 5,254 aircraft in still more powerful and improved variants. The great effectiveness of this combat plane is illustrated by the fact that, after the war, several hundred remained in active service in the units of the USAAF (with the designation B-26). They also continued their active career both in the Korean and the Vietnamese war.

The specifications for a new high performance well-armed ground attack plane were issued in 1940, and in June of the following year, Douglas signed an initial contract for the construction of three prototypes. These aircraft fulfilled various operative needs. The first (XA-26, maiden flight on July 10, 1942) was a traditional bomber with firing apparatus installed in the glazed nose. The second (XA-26A) was prepared as a night fighter, with four machine guns in a remote-controlled turret on the back of the fuselage and four 20 mm cannons in a fixed position in the belly. The third assumed the configuration of an attack plane and was armed with a 75 mm cannon installed in the nose.

The cycle of evaluations and comparative tests continued for a long time, and in the end, the third prototype was chosen as the first production variant (A-26B). The heavy cannon was eliminated, and in its place, six 12.7 mm machine guns were installed. This offensive armament was accompanied by four more weapons installed in pairs in two remote-controlled turrets on the back and belly of the aircraft respectively. Moreover, for special missions, it was possible to add another 10 machine guns: eight on the wings, in four containers, and two in external installations on the sides of the fuselage. Lastly, to complete this powerful armament, the bomb hold was capable of carrying up to 4,004 lb (1,814 kg) of bombs. Furthermore, in the case of an emergency, rockets, supplementary fuel tanks, or a further 2,002 lb (907 kg) of bombs could be installed in wing supports.

This veritable flying arsenal were first used in November 1944 on the European front, in the units of the 9th Air Force. The A-26Bs had their baptism of fire on November 19, and they proved to be the fastest bombers to be used by the USAAF in the conflict. Some months later, they also began their career on the Pacific front, with equally successful results.

Douglas completed 1,355 A-26Bs before production of the second version began (the A-26C, of which 1,091 were built). This marked a return to the configuration of a horizontal bomber with glazed nose and a reduction in the heavy armament on board. These Invaders went into service in 1945, and they took part in the last phase of the conflict.

color plate
Douglas A-26C 319th Bomber Group U.S.Army Air Force - Okinawa July 1945

Aircraft:	Douglas A-26B
Nation:	USA
Manufacturer:	Douglas Aircraft Co.
Type:	Bomber
Year:	1944
Engine:	2 Pratt & Whitney R-2800-27 Double Wasp, 18-cylinder radial, air-cooled, 2,000 hp each
Wingspan:	70 ft 1in (21.33 m)
Length:	50 ft 1 in (15.24 m)
Height:	18 ft 6 in (5.64 m)
Weight:	35,046 lb (15,876 kg)
Maximum speed:	353 mph (570 km/h) at 15,032 ft (4,570 m)
Ceiling:	22,154 ft (6,735 m)
Range:	1,399 miles (2,253 km)
Armament:	10 machine guns; 4,004 lb (1,814 kg) of bombs
Crew:	3

One of the earliest A-26As, still armed with a 75 mm cannon in the nose.

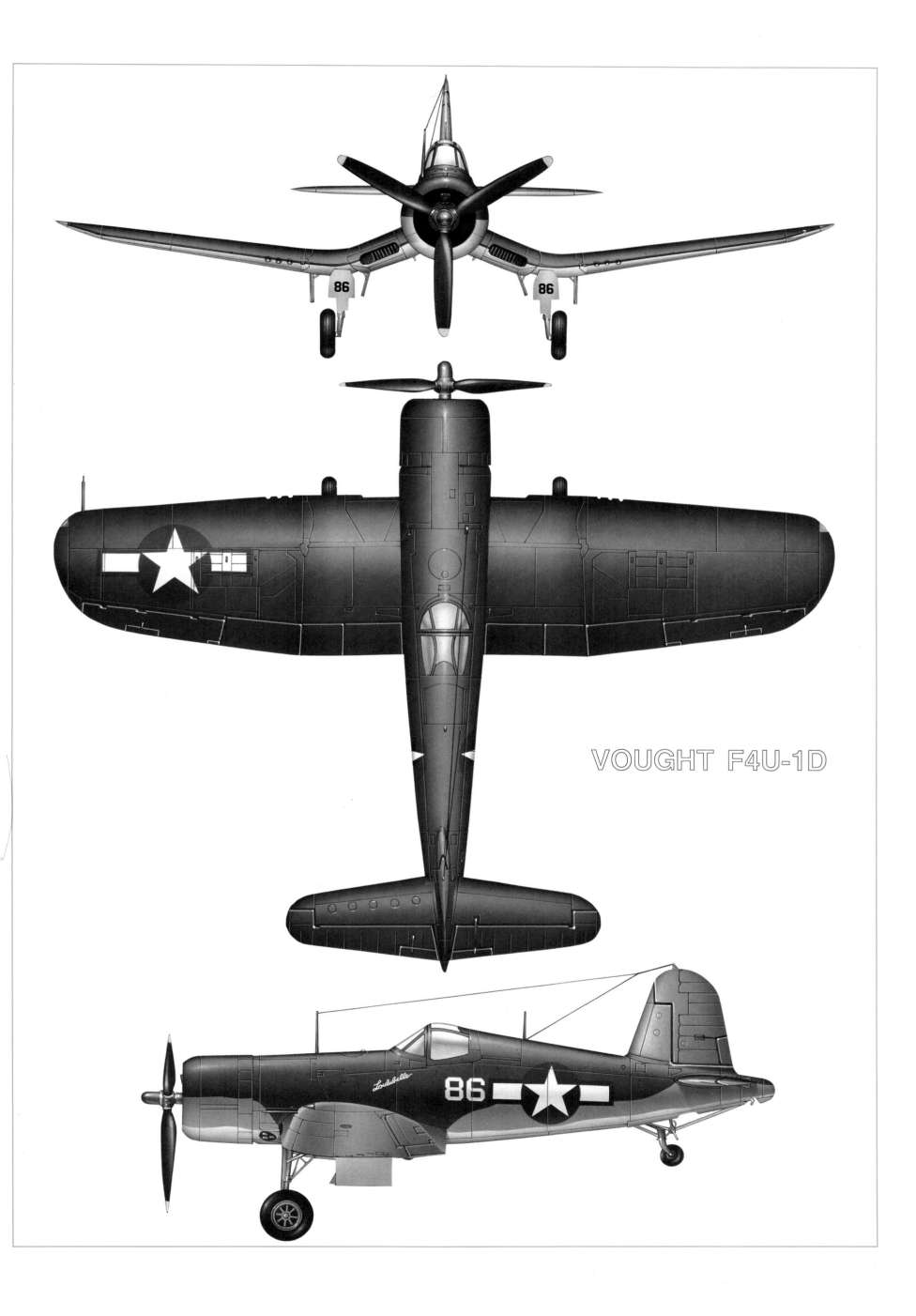

VOUGHT F4U-1D

A formation of F4U-1As in service with the British Navy.

The Vought F4U Corsair went down in history as one of the best fighters of the entire Second World War. With the Grumman F6F Hellcat, it shared the honor and the burden of the last two years of battle against Japan. In the course of the 64,051 missions (54,470 carried out from land bases and 9,581 from aircraft carriers) completed by the pilots of the U.S.Navy and the U.S.Marine Corps, the F4Us destroyed 2,140 enemy aircraft in combat, compared to only 189 losses, marking an incredible ratio of more than 11:1. Nevertheless, as these figures show, the Corsair passed about half of its career in the Pacific confined to land bases, despite its indisputable skills. This was due to the fact that for almost a year the U.S.Navy did not consider it suitable for use on board ship. However, the great potential of this powerful combat plane was eventually recognized. In fact, production continued without interruption for more than 10 years (until December 1952), and amounted to 12,571 aircraft in all. It continued to serve in the frontline of the units of the U.S.Navy until December 1954. Its career in the French Navy was even longer. The F4Us were used for another 10 years (until October 1964).

The Corsair was developed at the beginning of 1938, at the request of the U.S.Navy, which ordered the construction of the prototype of a new single-seater carrier-based fighter with advanced characteristics on June 30. Rex B. Beisel, Vought's chief designer, wanted to build the smallest possible airframe compatible with the most powerful engine available at the time, the Pratt & Whitney XR-2800 Double Wasp (a large 18-cylinder radial, generating 2,000 hp). The characteristic "inverted gull wing" shape was chosen, which also allowed for the adoption of a propeller with a large diameter. Such a propeller was capable of absorbing the remarkable engine power and shortening the legs of the forward landing gear to a maximum.

The XF4U-1 prototype took to the air for the first time on May 29, 1940, and right from the start its remarkable characteristics became apparent. During a transfer flight on October 1, the aircraft reached 403 mph (650 km/h), thus becoming the first American-produced fighter to go beyond the 400 mph (643,6 km/h) "limit." However, despite this brilliant performance, the preparation of the prototype proved to be long and laborious. An initial request was made for the strengthening of its armament. This modification made it necessary to move the fuel tanks on the wings and to add another in the fuselage. The pilot's seat was thus moved back by about three feet (90 cm), posing serious

visibility problems which were subsequently to create difficulties in the aircraft's qualification for carrier-based use.

On June 30, 1941, an initial contract for 584 F4U-1s was signed and the first production series aircraft appeared on October 30 of the following year. However, operations on board the aircraft carriers did not commence until April 1944, and the Corsair first went into service in the units of the Marines and then in the land based units of the U.S.Navy. In the course of the year, the Fleet Air Arm's F4Us went into frontline service on board the British aircraft carriers. The Fleet Air Arm received 2,012 aircraft (a further 370 going to the Royal New Zealand Air Force).

The aircraft of the initial version numbered 688 and they were followed on the assembly lines by 2,066 F4U-1As, with modifications to the engine, the landing gear and the cockpit canopy. The final change was carried out in order to improve the pilot's visibility. Subsequently, the principal variants were the F4U-1C (armed with four 20 mm cannons, 300 being built in all), and in 1944 the F4U-1D, with a more powerful engine and armament, of which Vought built 1,375. Vought's production was backed by that of Goodyear and Brewster. The former built 2,302 F4U-1Ds (designated FG-1D) and 1,704 F4U-1As (designated FG-1A), while the latter completed 735 F4U-1s with the designation F3A-1.

An F4U-1A of the VF 127 with 12 kill's markings.

color plate
Vought F4U-1D VMF 124 U.S.Marine squadron - New Guinea 1943. Personal aircraft of Major Greg Boyington (28 confirmed victories)

Aircraft:	Vought F4U-1D
Nation:	USA
Manufacturer:	United Aircraft Corp.
Type:	Fighter
Year:	1944
Engine:	Pratt & Whitney R-2800-8W Double Wasp, 18-cylinder radial, air-cooled, 2,250 hp
Wingspan:	41 ft (12.47 m)
Length:	33 ft 5 in (10.16 m)
Height:	16 ft 1 in (4.90 m)
Weight:	13,136 lb (5,951 kg)
Maximum speed:	424 mph (684 km/h) at 20,052 lb (6,096 m)
Ceiling:	33,990 lb (10,333 m)
Range:	1,014 miles (1,633 km)
Armament:	6 machine guns; 2,002 lb (907 kg) of bombs
Crew:	1

CURTISS SB2C-3

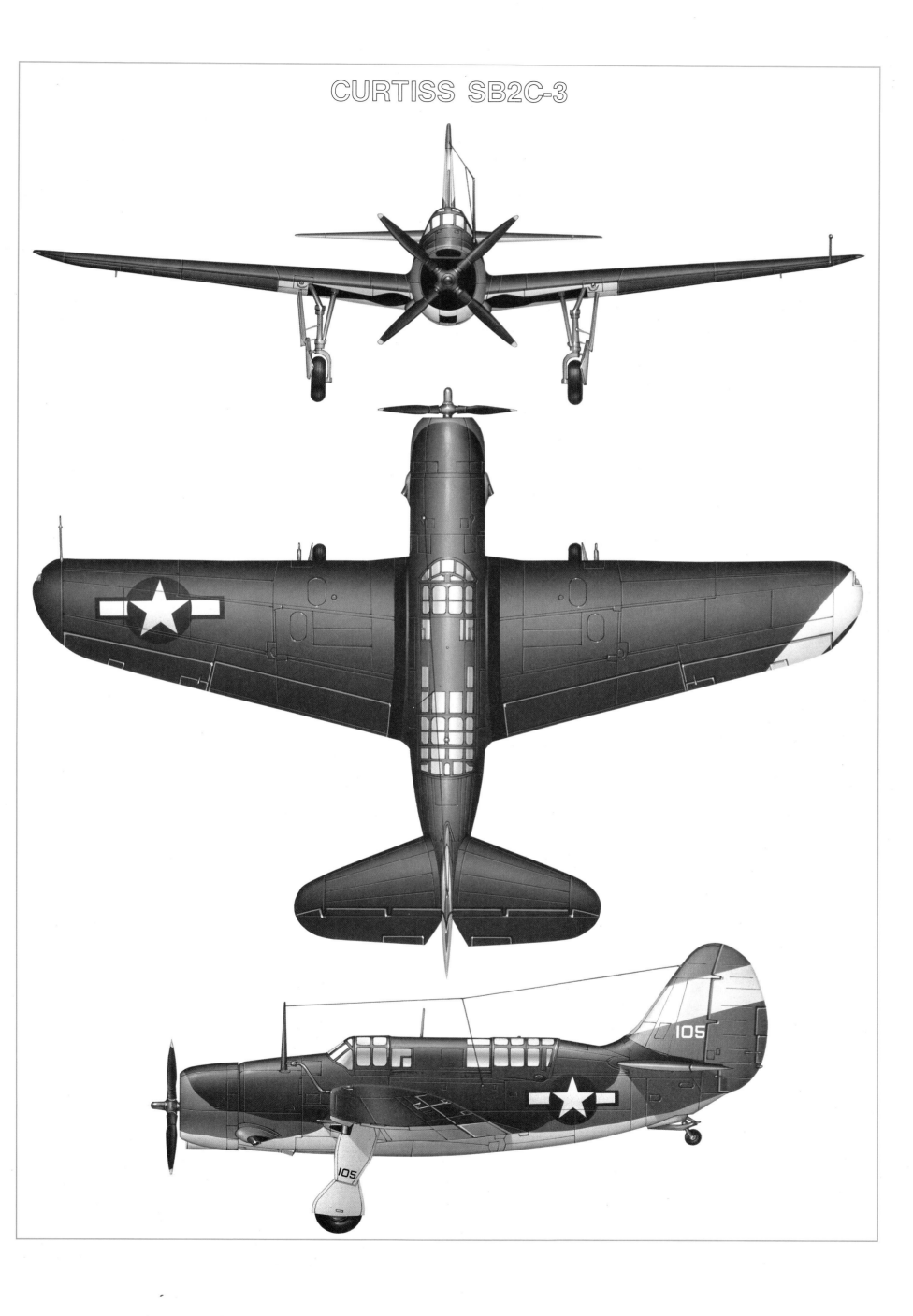

The SB2C Helldiver was the last combat plane that Curtiss built for the U.S.Navy and the Marines. Approximately 7,200 of these large and powerful single-engine carrier-based bombers were built in several versions. Beginning in November 1943, it backed the old SBD Dauntless as a dive-bomber, taking part in all air-sea operations until the end of the conflict. Many of the final production variants survived World War II and remained in service until the 1950s.

The Helldiver originated in 1938, when the U.S.Navy established a competition for a new carrier-based bomber-reconnaissance plane. Curtiss-Wright received an order for the construction of a prototype on May 15 of the following year and the aircraft, designated XSB2C-1 took to the air for the first time on December 18, 1940. It was not initially a success, in that it was destroyed in an accident at the beginning of January 1941, but the program went ahead nevertheless, sustained by orders for mass production which the Navy had already placed (November 29, 1940). However, the delays began to accumulate, not only due to the need to build another prototype, but also to carry out a whole series of modifications to the structure and equipment requested by the military technicians. These included an increase in fuel capacity and armament, the installation of self-sealing fuel tanks, and the enlarging of the surface area of the fins and rudder.

The first of the initial SB2C-1 series did not leave the factory until June 1942, and although deliveries to the units began in December, the aircraft did not become fully operative until the second half of the following year. The Helldiver made its debut in combat on November 11, 1943, with a bombing raid on Rabaul.

The SB2C was a large low-wing two-seater monoplane with retractable landing gear, and it was powered by a 1,700 hp Wright R-2600 radial engine. The defensive armament consisted of four machine guns on the wings (or two 20 mm cannons) and one or two similar weapons installed in a rear defensive position, at the observer's disposal. In addition, the bomb load could maintain a maximum of 2,002 lb (907 kg) of bombs installed in the hold and in supports below the wings.

In 1944, the second principal production version (SB2C-3, 1,112 built in all) appeared. It possessed a more powerful engine that drove a four-bladed propeller characterized by further detailed improvements. However, the major variant was the subsequent SB2C-4, in which the armament's flexibility was increased by the installation of four racks beneath the wings to hold a similar number of 127 mm rockets or 501 lb (227 kg) of bombs. Curtiss alone built almost 2,000 of this version of the Helldiver. In fact, to sustain the increasing demands of the U.S.Navy, the production program was widened to include the participation of the Canadian companies Fairchild Aircraft Ltd. in Longueil, and the Canadian Car & Foundry in Montreal. These two firms built on license 300 and 894 aircraft respectively in several variants, designated with the characteristic abbreviation of SBF and SBW. The final version was the SB2C-5, which appeared in the early month of 1945, and was characterized mainly by an increase in fuel capacity. 970 were built in all.

In the course of the conflict the Helldivers were employed almost exclusively by the U.S.Navy.

Only 26 (that were never used) were sent to Great Britain, while the Marines took most of the 900 aircraft specially built for the Army aviation, that had ordered them in April 1941. They were designated A-25A and then SB2C-1A.

---

color plate

Curtiss SB2C-3 VB-9 aircraft carrier *Lexington* U.S.Navy Air Force - Pacific sea, February 1945

Aircraft:	Curtiss SB2C-1
Nation:	USA
Manufacturer:	Curtiss-Wright Corp.
Type:	Bomber
Year:	1943
Engine:	Wright R-2600-8 Cyclone, 14-cylinder radial, air-cooled, 1,700 hp
Wingspan:	49 ft 10 in (15.16 m)
Length:	36 ft 9 in (11.18 m)
Height:	13 ft 2 in (4.01 m)
Weight:	16,637 lb (7,537 kg)
Maximum speed:	280 mph (452 km/h) at 16,743 ft (5,090 m)
Ceiling:	25,164 ft (7,650 m)
Range:	1,108 miles (1,785 km)
Armament:	2 x 20 mm cannons; 2 machine guns; 2,002 lb (907 kg) of bombs
Crew:	2

An SB2C-1 taking off from an aircraft-carrier during operations in the Pacific.

An SB2C-4 employed as a torpedo plane. This was the Helldiver's major variant.

THE UNITED STATES OF AMERICA

Following the decisive turning point at Midway, in which the Americans struck the first hard blow against the supremacy of the Empire of the Rising Sun, the war against Japan entered its final phase in the summer of 1944. Apart from the massive offensive which the Allied forces were conducting to reconquer the territories occupied by the enemy, the strategic factor that made this evolution of the conflict possible was the American possession of the Mariana archipelago. In fact, it was from these islands in the middle of the Pacific, that the Americans transferred the attack directly onto Japanese territory, thanks to the availability of the new Boeing B-29 strategic bombers.

These powerful aircraft had begun their career on June 5, 1944, from bases located in China. Ten days later, they carried out the first bombing raid on Japan, with an attack on the steel plants at Kyushu. This marked the beginning of increasingly intensive and devastating missions which, from November 24, were carried out from the Mariana Island bases. In fact, that very day, 111 B-29s, of the 73rd Bomb Wing of the USAAF's XXI Bomber Command, completed their first mission on Tokyo, repeating with greater military importance the daring and symbolic raid that had been carried out by Doolittle's B-25s on April 18, 1942.

The enormous development which the aeronautical weapon underwent in the United States during World War II can be summed up by these two dates. In fact, in the intervening period, the best combat planes to be constructed by the American aeronautical industry appeared: aircraft such as the P-51 Mustang, the P-47 Thunderbolt, the F6F Hellcat, and the F4U Corsair in the fighter sector, or such as the final variants of the B-17s and B-24s (as well as the B-29 itself) in that of the bombers. Not only did these aircraft make a decisive contribution to the course of the war, but they also went down in the history of aviation as outstanding champions of aeronautical technology.

The great effort in the Pacific and in Europe was made possible only by the huge potential of the American industrial network which, in the last years of the conflict, produced record quantities. This reached a peak in 1944, when 96,318 aircraft (including 38,873 fighters and 35,003 bombers; 16,331 of the latter were four-engined and 10,058 were two-engined) and 256,911 engines were built.

The production rise is evident when compared to the previous years. In 1941, aeronautical production had amounted to 19,445 aircraft of all types and 58,181 engines; the following year, which was still a transitional one as far as the strengthening of the USAAF (U.S.Army Air Forces) and the U.S.Navy aviation were concerned, a first, abrupt leap was recorded, with 47,836 aircraft (including 10,769 fighters and 12,627 bombers of which 2,615 were four-engined and 7,247 were two-engined) and 138,089 engines were constructed.

In 1943, aeronautical production leapt to 85,898 aircraft of all types (23,988 fighters, 29,355 bombers, of which 9,615 were four-engined and 10,361 two-engined), while the number of engines produced reached a total of 227,116.

Chronology

1943

January 9. The prototype of the Lockheed L-049 Constellation, destined to go into service in the USAAF as the C-69, takes to the air. The military career of this outstanding transport plane was accompanied by a commercial one after the war, which was equally long and intensive. Up till 1959, a total of 856 were built in several versions.

February 11. First mission (carried out by the VMF-127 Squadron of the Marines) employing the new Chance Vought F4U Corsair fighter, one of the protagonists of the American recovery in the Pacific. In all, 12,681 were built in numerous versions.

June 1. At Marietta, in Georgia, the 58th Very Heavy Bombardment Wing of the USAAF is founded, and was to be equipped with the new B-29 Superfortresses. The unit was established to carry out strategic attacks on Japan.

1944

January 8. The prototype of the Lockheed XP-80 Shooting Star, the first American single-seater jet fighter, takes to the air at Muroc Dry Lake, in California. It was to go into service once the war was over and was widely used in the Korean conflict.

June 5. The Boeing B-29s carry out their first combat mission from bases on Chinese territory: a raid on the railway warehouses in Bangkok.

June 15. The first strategic bombing raid on Japan is carried out by 68 B-29s based at Chengtu, in China. The target was the steel plants in Kyushu. It occurred two years after the purely symbolic one carried out by Doolittle's B-25s on April 18, 1942.

July 5. The Northrop MX-324, the first rocket aircraft to be built in the United States, makes its maiden flight.

November 24. First raid on Tokyo, carried out by the B-29s based in the Mariana Islands. Up till August 6, 1945, the B-29s specialized in raids with incendiary bombs, initially by day, and then by night at low altitude.

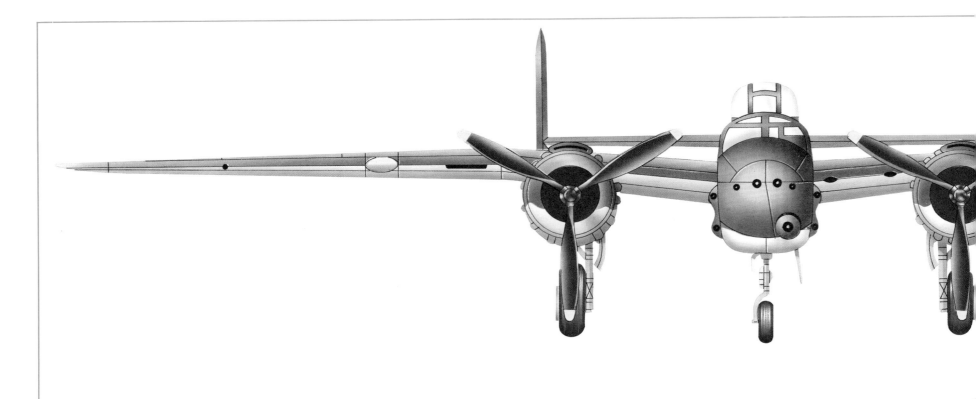

NORTH AMERICAN B-25H

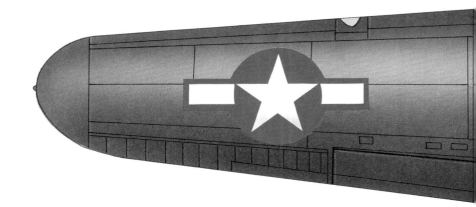

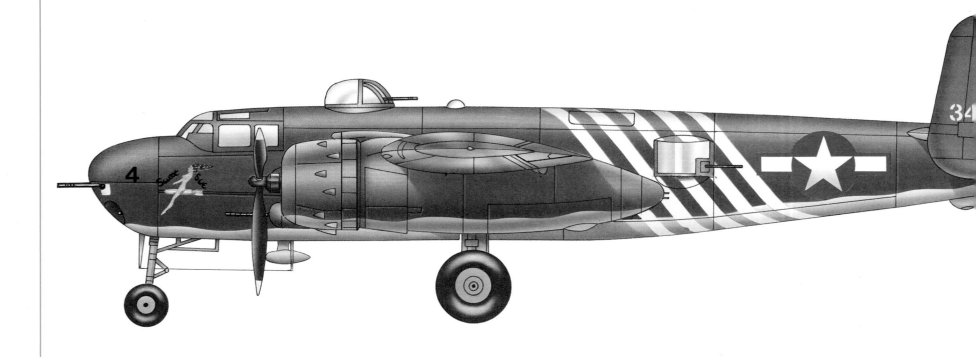

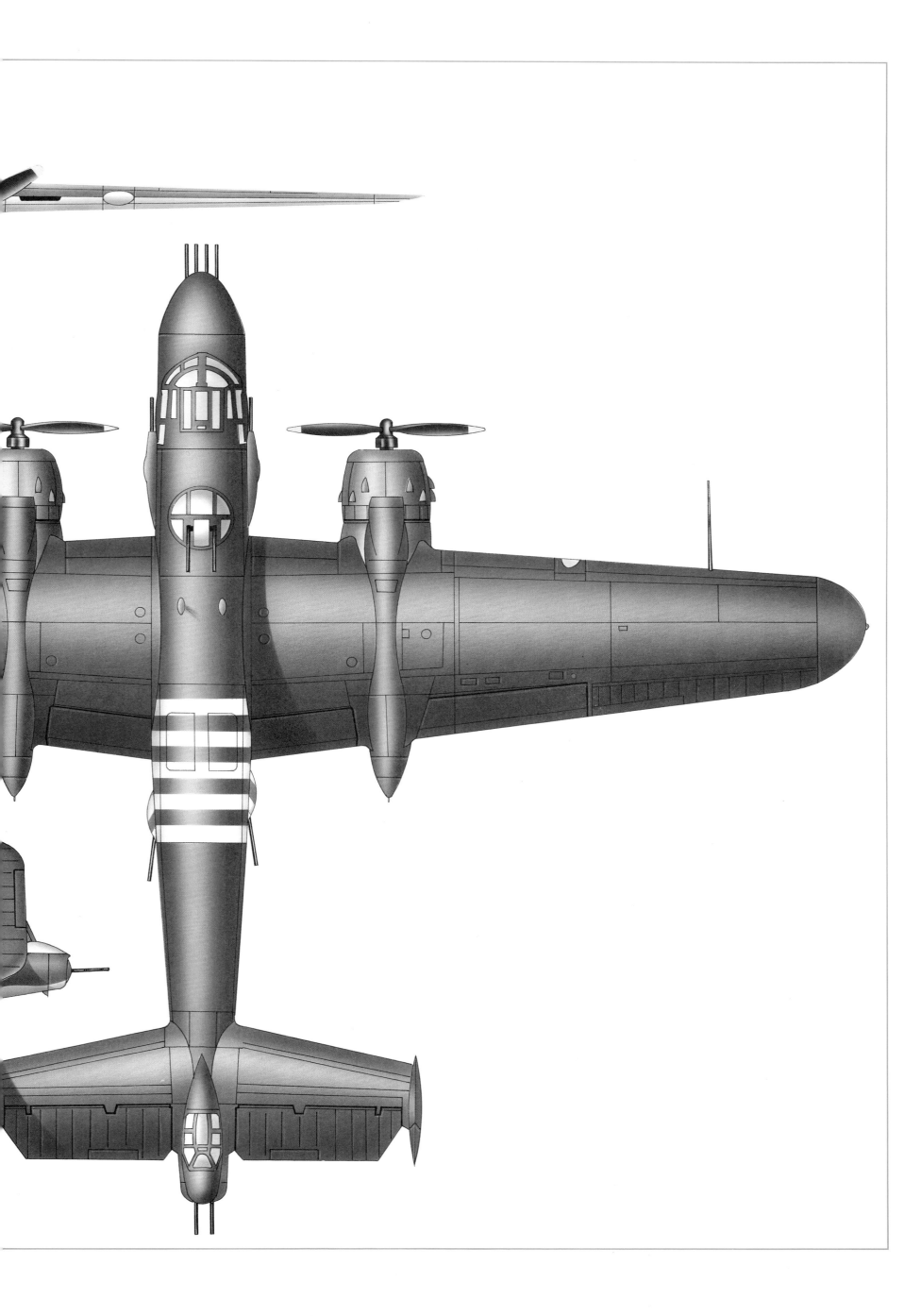

Created back in 1938, more than 11,000 North American B-25 Mitchells were built between 1940 and 1945. The aircraft had a long and intensive career that lasted well beyond World War II. This occurred due to continuous modernization and strengthening which exploited to the full this two-engine aircraft's great potential. The Mitchell went down in history as one of the best bombers of the war.

The first versions to be produced in any number were the B-25C and B-25D, which were delivered at the end of 1941, and of which 1,619 and 2,290 were built respectively. In 1942, it was in fact as a result of modifications carried out on three experimental prototypes of the B-25C that the subsequent G variant came into being. This was subjected to a radical change in armament, the first step towards the subsequent developments that were to transform the Mitchell into a veritable flying cruiser: the installation in the nose of a 75 mm caliber M4 cannon. This weapon could fire 21 bullets — each of which weighed 15 lb (6.81 kg) — and its intended use was to be in anti-shipping attacks, especially in operations in the Pacific.

405 B-25Gs were built in all, but due to practical problems in loading and firing the cannon, production was altered in favor of the subsequent H version (1,000 built in all). This was a remarkable improvement. In this aircraft, the M4 cannon was replaced by a lighter, more modern weapon (the T-13E1), the crew was reduced to five members, and the offensive armament was reinforced still further by the installation of eight heavy machine guns in the fuselage's front section, in addition to the six for the defense of the side, back and rear sections. This impressive firing power (which could be integrated with a maximum of eight rockets installed in racks beneath the wings), together with the "normal" bomb load contained in the hold, made the Mitchell a formidable weapon. The first B-25Hs arrived on the Pacific front in February 1944, and following a few months of acclimatization, they went into action with great success against Japanese land and sea traffic. The heavy armament installed in the nose proved to be particularly effective especially in anti-shipping attacks.

The next major production version, the B-25J (this was built in the greatest number: 4,390 out of total 4,805 ordered of which 295 were sent to Great Britain) embodied the final evolution of the airframe. This variant initially marked a return to the classic structure of a horizontal bomber equipped with glazed nose, and

then to that of ground attack plane with basic armament consisting of 12 machine guns and an enlarged crew of six men.

During the conflict, the two-engine North American operated on all fronts and without interruption until the final day of the war, although the principal theater of war, as far as the aircraft of the USAAF and the U.S.Navy were concerned, was that of the Pacific. In this sector, the B-25s carried out an invaluable role, guaranteeing support to the land forces in the slow and difficult advance until the battle for Okinawa. In Europe, the USAAF's Mitchells were flanked by those of the British RAF and the aircraft of a Free French bombing group. Starting with the Allied landings in Morocco and Algeria, the B-25s carried out a total of 63,177 missions, releasing 84,980 tons of bombs and shooting down 193 enemy aircraft.

The third great consumer of the B-25, after the USAAF and the RAF, was the U.S.Navy which, from January 1943 onward, received 50 PBJ-1Cs (equivalent to the B-25C), 152 PBJ-1Ds (B-25D), one PBJ-1G (B-25G), 248 PBJ-1Hs (B-25H) and 225 PBJ-1Js (B-25J).

color plate

North American B-25H 1st Air Command Group 10th Air Force USAAF - Hailakandi, India, 1944

Aircraft:	North American B-25H
Nation:	USA
Manufacturer:	North American Aviation Inc.
Type:	Bomber
Year:	1944
Engine:	2 Wright R-2600-13 Cyclone, 14-cylinder radial, air-cooled, 1,724 hp each
Wingspan:	67 ft 11 in (20.60 m)
Length:	51 ft 1 in (15.54 m)
Height:	15 ft 9 in (4.80 m)
Weight:	37,198 lb (16,351 kg)
Maximum speed:	274 mph (442 km/h) at 13,026 ft (3,960 m)
Ceiling:	23,865 ft (7,255 m)
Range:	1,350 miles (2,173 km)
Armament:	1 x 75 mm cannon; 14 machine guns; 3,004 lb (1,361 kg) of bombs
Crew:	5

A formation of North American B-25 in flight.

BELL P-63A

The final exponent of the family of P-39 Airacobras, the P-63 Kingcobra, differed from its predecessors not only in its more carefully studied aerodynamics, its greater size, and its more powerful Allison engine, but above all to the fact that it had been conceived initially as a fighter-bomber for tactical support. The P-63 carried out this role excellently, although the USAAF never used it in combat. In fact, of the 3,303 aircraft that were built, the majority (2,421) were sent to the Soviet Union. Another 300 were delivered to the Free French units. These aircraft were used by American military aviation only as trainers or targets. A special variant (RP-63) was built expressly for this purpose. This model possessed no armament and had been provided with reinforced covering in order to withstand the impact of the special shattering bullets used during training. Every hit made a red light on the wing tips blink.

The Kingcobra project was launched in the same period as the initial development of the P-39. The aim was to introduce the P-39's aerodynamic improvements to the other aircraft. Three experimental aircraft were built (XP-39E). They possessed the P-39D's fuselage and a wing provided with a laminar profile and squared tips; the tail planes were also modified. The tests went ahead successfully, stimulating the request for series production, with the designation P-76.

However, this program was cancelled after a few months. Instead, it was decided to build a larger and more powerful version of the aircraft, to be used as a fighter-bomber and tactical support fighter. In June 1941, two XP-63 prototypes were ordered, and they took to the air on December 7 and February 5, 1943, respectively. They were fitted with a 1,325 hp Allison V-1710-47 engine that drove a four-bladed metal variable-pitch propeller. During tests, the two aircraft crashed and a third prototype (XP-63A) had to be built. It made its maiden flight on April 26, 1943. In the meantime, the first production order had been placed for 1,725 aircraft (on September 29, 1942) and the first deliveries of the initial P-63A version commenced in October.

These Kingcobras were followed by 1,227 of the second principal variant, the P-63C (first delivered in January 1945), in which, as well as aerodynamic modifications an Allison V-1710-117 engine was fitted. This could generate 1,825 hp in an emergency, thanks to a water injection system. Besides these basic models, numerous subseries were built, differing from each other in their equipment (carrying supplementary fuel tanks) and offensive armament. Lastly, mention should be made of the only P-63D, characterized by

An XP-63D with modified canopy and cannon in the propeller hub.

a greater wingspan, drop canopy and 1,425 hp Allison V-1710-109 engine, and thirteen P-63Es, similar to the previous models, but with a traditional canopy. No fewer than 2,930 of these aircraft delivered in May 1945, were ordered before the course of the war led to their cancellation.

color plate
Bell P-63A Soviet Air Force - 1944

Aircraft:	Bell P-63A Kingcobra
Nation:	USA
Manufacturer:	Bell Aircraft Corp.
Type:	Fighter
Year:	1943
Engine:	Allison V-1710-95, 12-cylinder .V, liquid-cooled, 1,325 hp
Wingspan:	38 ft 5 in (11.68 m)
Length:	32 ft 11 in (9.96 m)
Height:	12 ft 5 in (3.84 m)
Weight:	10,514 lb (4,763 kg)
Maximum speed:	409 mph (660 km/h) at 25,065 ft (7,620 m)
Ceiling:	43,111 ft (13,106 m)
Range:	449 miles (724 km)
Armament:	1 x 37 mm cannon; 4 machine guns; 523 lb (237 kg) of bombs
Crew:	1

A Kingcobra that was modified as an experiment, with skis being adopted instead of wheels.

An E series Kingcobra characterized by substantial modifications to the rear end of the fuselage.

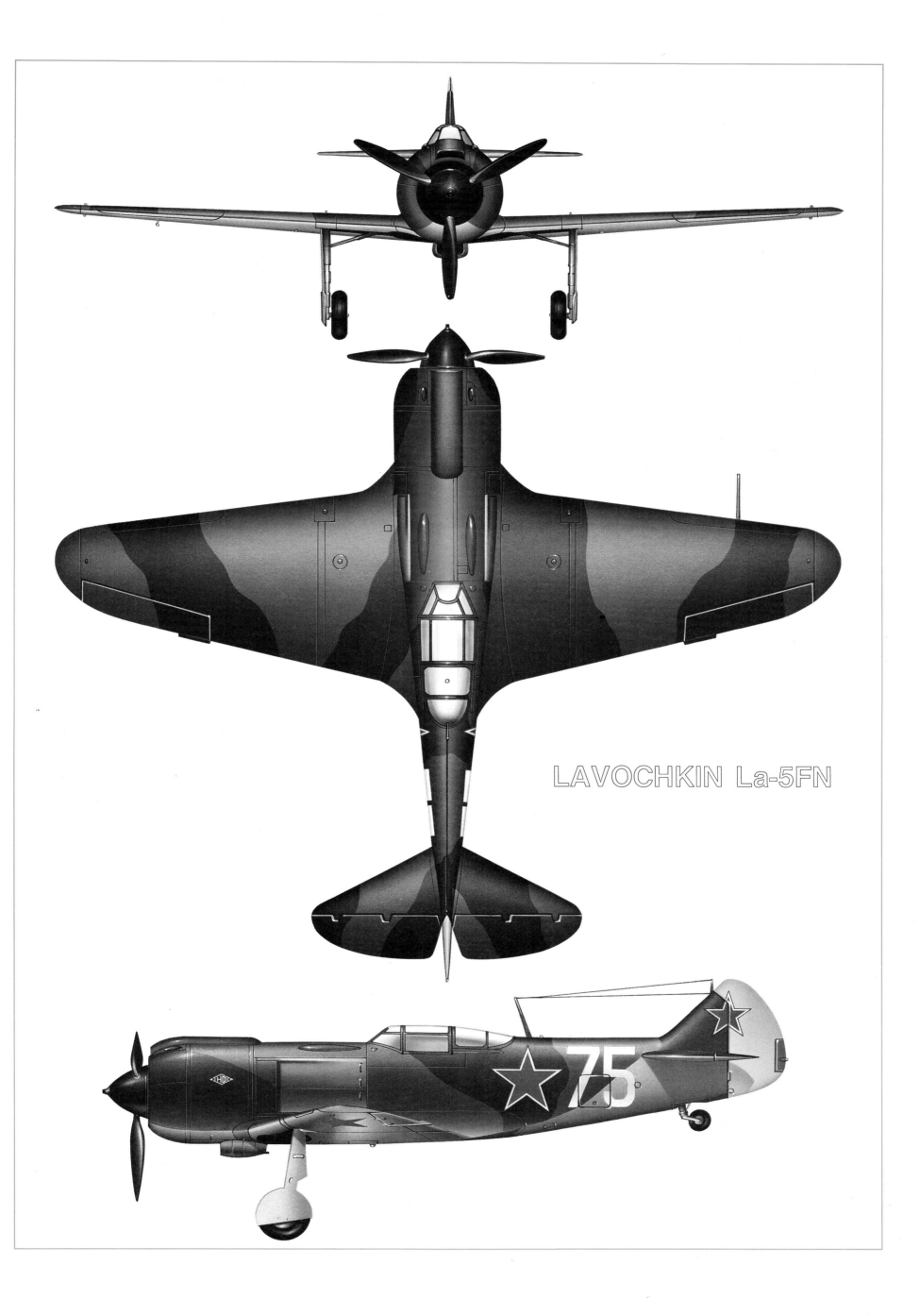

LAVOCHKIN La-5FN

LAVOCHKIN La-5

The prolific family of combat planes built in the Soviet Union by Semyon Alexseyevich Lavochkin (its first notable exponents were the LaGG-1 and the LaGG-3) was enriched toward the end of 1941, by a new version, in which the Russian technician succeeded in expressing the full potential of his initial project. The factor which gave a new life to the mediocre LaGG-3 was the installation of a radically new engine, the 1,600 hp Shvetsov M.82 radial. When this engine was installed in place of the liquid-cooled Klimov M.105P, it transformed the aircraft into a first-class machine: the La-5, as it was designated, became one of the best Soviet fighters of the entire conflict.

Right from the first tests, which began toward the end of March 1942, it became clear that the new variant was a marked improvement over the basic model: the more powerful engine and lighter weight (obtained by eliminating the cooling systems) compensated for the increase in the front section (and the consequently greater aerodynamic resistance) due to the space occupied by the large double radial engine. The new variant also allowed for a remarkable increase in performance which, in horizontal speed alone, improved by almost 25 mph (40 km/h). The new power plant was installed in the LaGG-3 in May 1942. This modification gave rise to a transitional aircraft, designated LaGG-5, which was replaced a few weeks later by the definitive La-5 model. In this aircraft, the fuselage rear trunk was lowered in order to allow for the installation of a canopy providing 360° visibility.

The new fighters were sent immediately to the units, and production continued at a fast rate. By the time of the Battle of Stalingrad, the La-5 was being used on the whole front. Nevertheless, the aircraft still had to be perfected. Its performance could not be compared with that of its principal German rival, the Messerschmitt Bf.109 G. Consequently, Lavochkin carried out a series of studies to improve the aircraft's characteristics and his work led to the creation of a second variant (La-5FN), which became the principal production model. As well as the adoption of M.82FN direct injection engine (capable of generating 1,700 hp) and overall aerodynamic improvements, the designer changed from an entirely wood airframe to one that was mixed (metallic spars were used for the wings). In addition, he improved the control surfaces, thus decidedly increasing the fighter's maneuverability. The La-5FN was delivered to the units in 1943. By October 1944, about 10,000 had been completed. These remained in service for the rest of the war.

A two-seater training version was also built (designated La-5UTI, it appeared in August 1943), characterized by the installation of two cockpits (placed close together) with separate sliding canopies. These aircraft were distributed to the units and proved extremely useful in training pilots in what perhaps remained the Lavochkin fighter's only serious fault: its difficult handling during takeoff and landing. In the spring of 1944, the first aircraft of a new, improved, and more powerful variant began to leave the assembly lines. This was the La-7 which served in its turn for the subsequent developments that resulted in the La-11. The latter appeared immediately after the war. It was the only fighter in the Soviet Air Force to have a piston engine.

color plate

Lavochkin La-5FN Soviet Air Force - Poland and Berlin, 1944-45. Personal aircraft of Squadron Commander Vitali Ivanovich Popkov, "Double Hero of the Soviet Union"

Aircraft:	Lavochkin La-5FN
Nation:	USSR
Manufacturer:	State Industries
Type:	Fighter
Year:	1943
Engine:	Shvetsov M.82FN, 14-cylinder radial, air-cooled, 1,700 hp
Wingspan:	32 ft 2 in (9.80 m)
Length:	28 ft 3 in (8.60 m)
Height:	8 ft 4 in (2.54 m)
Weight:	7,417 lb (3,360 kg)
Maximum speed:	401 mph (647 km/h) at 16,447 ft (5,000 m)
Ceiling:	31,250 ft (9,500 m)
Range:	475 miles (765 km)
Armament:	2 x 20 mm cannons; 441 lb (200 kg) of bombs
Crew:	1

A Lavochkin La-7 in flight with its canopy open.

THE SOVIET UNION

After a huge reorganization of the Soviet industrial network which occurred in the winter of 1941-1942, the years which followed were characterized by a full productive recovery. In 1943, a total of 35,000 aircraft and 49,000 engines came off the assembly lines, while 40,300 aircraft of all types were completed in 1944. This marked a great step forward, considering that in 1941, although a total of 15,735 aircraft were built, production had literally collapsed in the second half of the year and in the early months of 1942 (1,039 aircraft were completed in January, 915 in February, and 1,647 in March), concluding with a total of 25,400 aircraft and 38,000 engines.

However, the recovery in the aeronautical field was not only quantitative, but also primarily qualitative, with the appearance of aircraft that were the fruit of new projects, especially in the fighter sector and that of the ground attack planes. These initially contributed to redressing the balance in regard to the Luftwaffe, and subsequently to marking a definitive supremacy in the air.

At the same time, the process of transforming the aeronautical industry continued with the increasingly repeated introduction of the mechanization and rationalization of the assembly lines and the productive units. In addition the gradual transition from the traditional methods of wood construction to more modern ones using metal (for the airframes, as well as the covering) revolutionized the industry. This entire potential was directly immersed in the tumult of the war, initially, to oppose the threat of the immediate enemy, Germany, and subsequently, to launch the final phase of reconquering the occupied territories and of advancing on Germany itself.

However, the massive contribution, in terms of aircraft and materials by the other Allies, was essential to this process. In the aeronautical field, especially, from 1941 to 1945, the United States alone sent the Soviet Union approximately 15,000 aircraft of all types and no less than 500 million dollars in machinery, plants, and raw materials (steel, copper and aluminum).

The result was a further leap forward as far as the Soviet aeronautical industry was concerned.

Therefore, it was able not only to build the enormous total of 125,000 aircraft in the course of the entire conflict, reaching a production rate of 41,800 aircraft per year in 1945, but also to acquire a full autonomy and a total competitiveness, indispensable requisites for the remarkable developments that were to take place immediately after the war.

Chronology

1943

August. The first Tupolev Tu-2s come off the assembly lines. This two-engine aircraft was to become the second most important medium bomber to be built in the Soviet Union. A total of 2,527 of these aircraft were built in all, 1,111 during World War II. It remained in service until the 1950s.

1944

Spring. The first Lavochkin La-7s begin to come off the assembly lines. The already excellent characteristics of this aircraft's predecessor, the La-5, were improved still further and the La-7 assisted in the subsequent developments that were to culminate in the La-11 immediately after the war.

August. Series production of the Ilyushin Il-10 Sturmovik, the final evolution of the famous Il-2 assault plane, is launched. Although it retained the basic design of its predecessor, from many points of view, this aircraft embodied an entirely new project. It was characterized by an all-metal airframe, remarkable aerodynamic improvements and modifications in the power plant and main landing gear. Series production of the Il-10 ceased more than ten years later, after almost 5,000 aircraft had been completed.

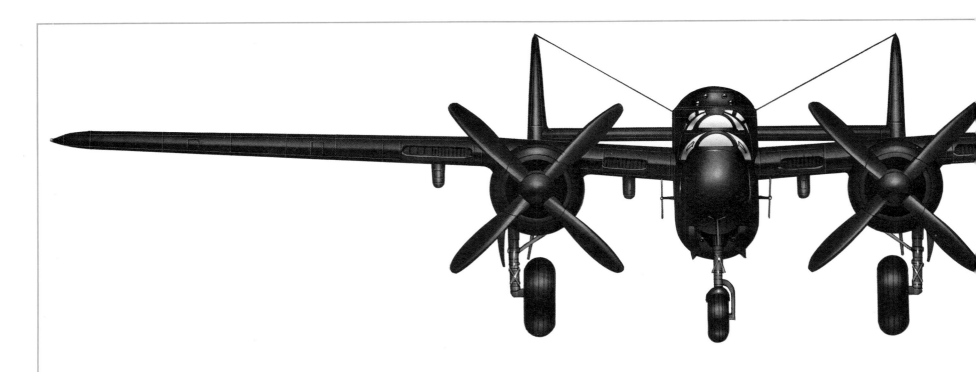

NORTHROP P-61B

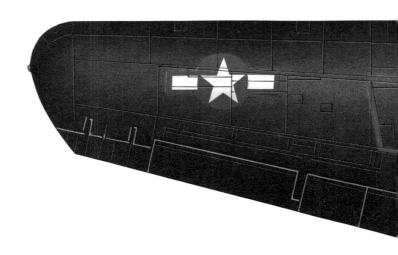

Lady in the Dark

2397

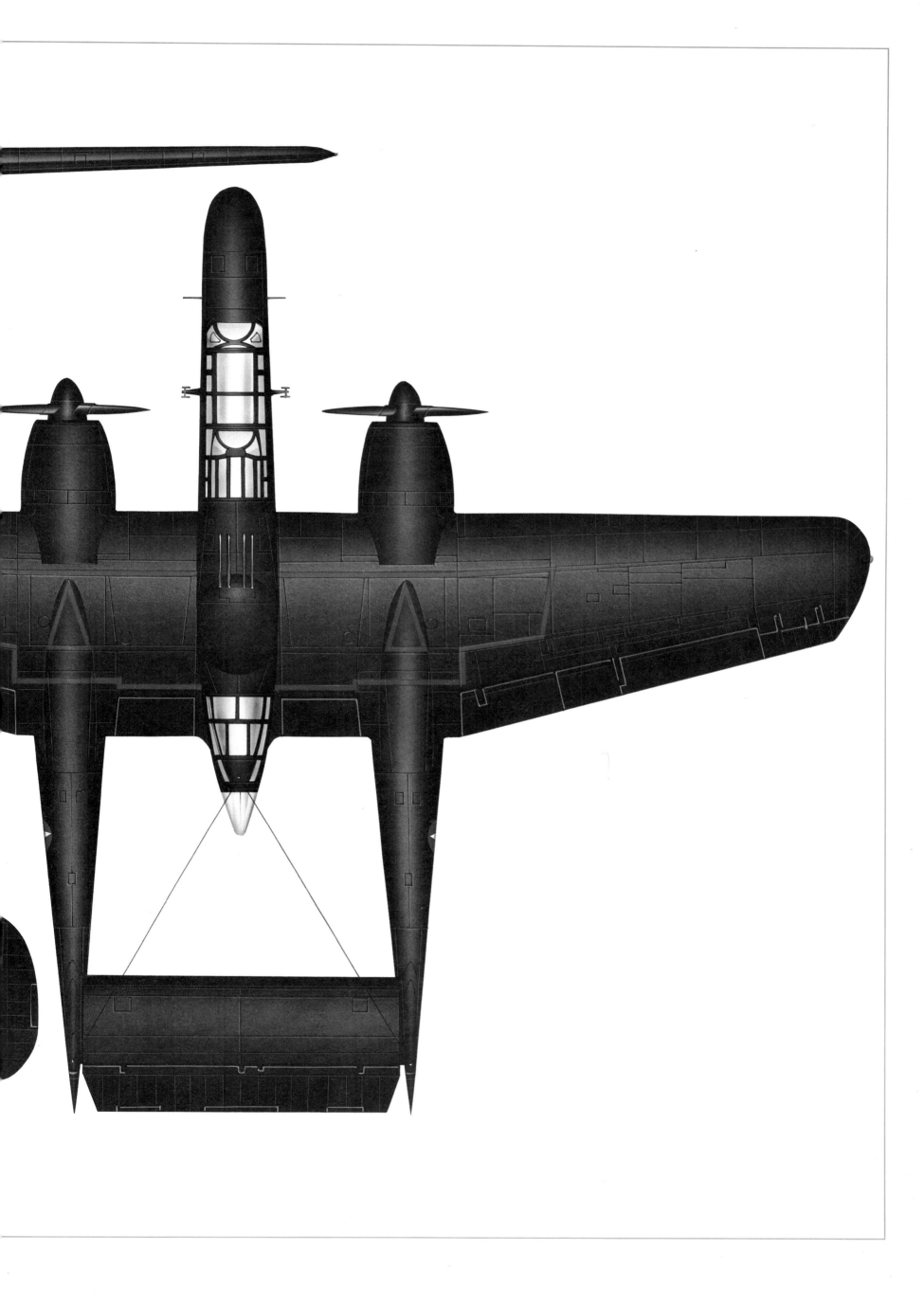

The P-61 Black Widow was not only the largest, heaviest and most powerful fighter of the entire war, but it was also the only night fighter designed as such by the American aeronautical industry. It proved to be one of the best aircraft in this category. Although designed in 1940, the P-61 did not go into action until the last year of the war, due to a long and complex preparation concerning its radar apparatus. Just over 700 were built in three principal versions. Some of them, in the photoreconnaissance version, survived the war and remained in active service until 1952.

It was in 1940, after the reports of a special commission, sent to Great Britain to evaluate the operative needs of the conflict, had been received that the USAAF strongly felt the need for a valid night fighter with radar apparatus that was being developed at the time. On October 2, highly secret specifications were issued for an aircraft of this type, and just over a month later, on November 5, Northrop, which was already working on a design of this kind, submitted its own project to the military authorities. The proposal was accepted and the program launched within a brief space of time. On January 11, 1941, two XP-61 prototypes were ordered, followed by 13 pre-series YP-61s on March 10, meant for operative evaluation tests. On September 1, the first order, for 150 series aircraft, was placed.

The project was developed bearing in mind these extremely short deadlines and the first prototype took to the air on May 21, 1942. The Black Widow (named after the deadly spider found in the American desert) was a large high-wing two-engine aircraft with forward tricycle landing gear. It was powered by a pair of Pratt & Whitney Double Wasp radial engines, each generating 2,000 hp and driving four-blade metal variable-pitch propellers. In addition it was characterized by double tail beams, which lengthened the engine fairings and supported the horizontal and vertical fins. The aircraft was provided with a specific system of control surfaces which notably increased its maneuverability. The radar apparatus (based upon British projects and developed by the Massachusetts Institute of Technology) was installed in the nose. The armament consisted of four 20 mm cannons fixed in the belly pod and a similar number of 12.7 mm machine guns installed in a remote-controlled turret on the aircraft's back.

Deliveries of the initial production series aircraft (P-61A) began in October 1943, and these became operative the following year, going into action in the spring and summer, both on the European and Pacific fronts. Beginning in August 1944, the first of the second variant (P-61B, 450 built in all) were delivered. In this aircraft, the Black Widow's already powerful armament was further increased with the installation of wing supports capable of carrying four 1,602 lb (726 kg) bombs or supplementary fuel tanks containing 340 gallons (1,363 liters). The last major production variant was the P-61C, strengthened above all in the engines. The Pratt & Whitney R-2800-73s with supercharger, capable of generating 2,839 hp in an emergency was installed. Only 41 of the latter were built, out of an order for 517, and they were delivered in July 1945.

In the immediate post-war years another variant appeared, intended for use as a photoreconnaissance, and only 36 were built in all. Designated F-15A Reporter, the aircraft had a modified fuselage and was characterized by its lack of radar equipment and armament. Moreover, it had remarkable qualities: a maximum speed of 440 mph (708 km/h), a 41,101 ft (12,495 m) tangent, and a range of 3,997 miles (6,437 km). This variant was the last to withdrawn from service.

A long nose P-61B with its characteristic black paint.

color plate

Northrop P-61B 548th Night Fighter Squadron 7th Air Force U.S.Army Air Force - Ryukyu Island August 1945. This aircraft shot down the last plane in World War II

Aircraft:	Northrop P-61B
Nation:	USA
Manufacturer:	Northrop Aircraft Inc.
Type:	Night fighter
Year:	1944
Engine:	2 Pratt & Whitney R-2800-65 Double Wasp, 18-cylinder radial, air-cooled, 2,000 hp each
Wingspan:	66 ft 1 in (20.11 m)
Length:	49 ft 7 in (15.11 m)
Height:	14 ft 8 in (4.47 m)
Weight:	29,739 lb (13,472 kg)
Maximum speed:	365 mph (589 km/h) at 20,052 ft (6,096 m)
Ceiling:	33,187 ft (10,089 m)
Range:	2,998 miles (4,828 km)
Armament:	4 x 20 mm cannons; 4 machine guns; 6,410 lb (2,904 kg) of bombs
Crew:	3

A P-61A with short nose. On the back of the fuselage there are four fixed 12.7 mm weapons.

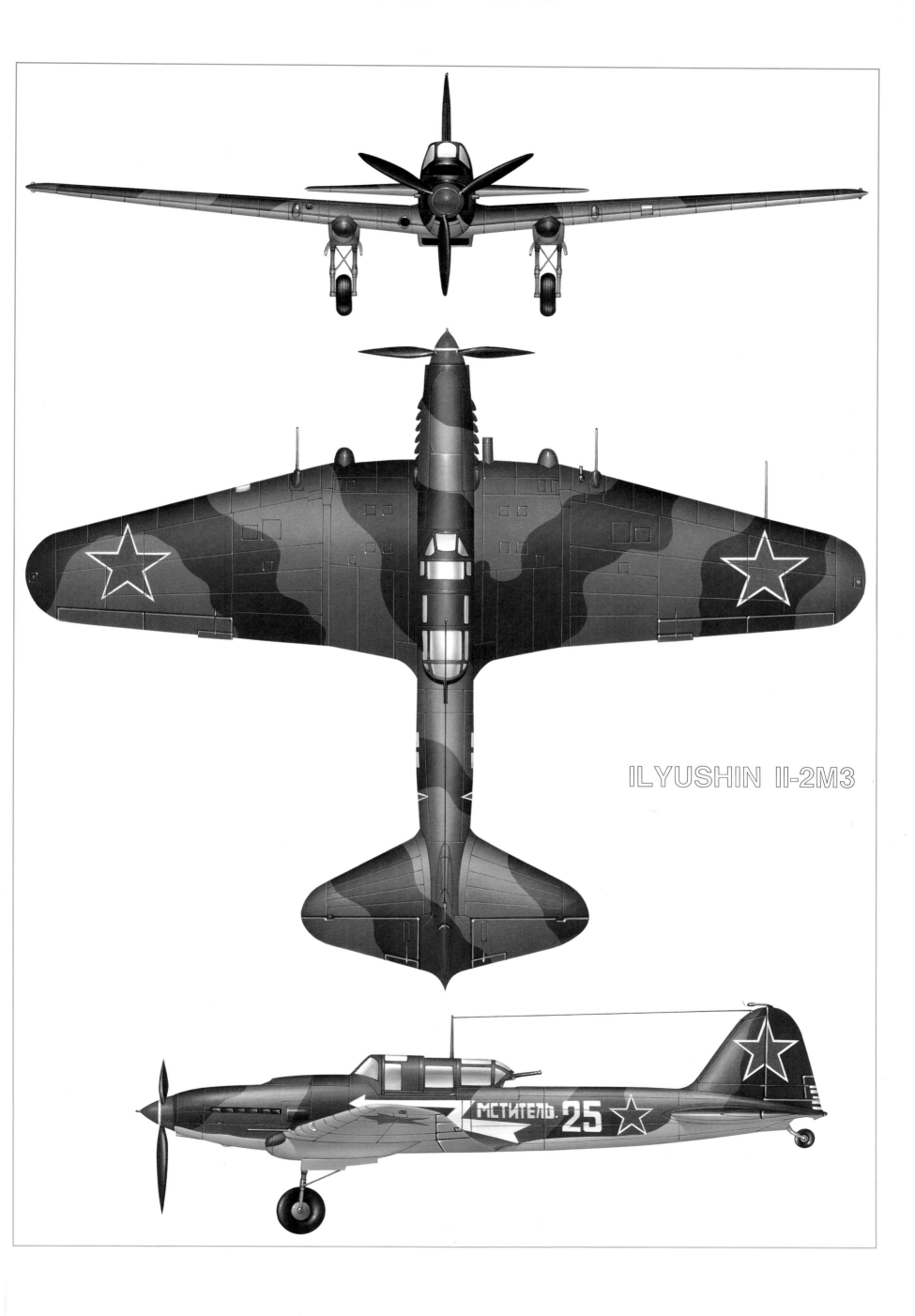

ILYUSHIN Il-2M3

One of the most effective families of combat planes built in the Soviet Union during World War II was that which gave rise to the Ilyushin Sturmoviks. Starting with the initial Il-2 model of 1940, until the final Il-10 variant of 1944, these strong and capable single-engine ground attack planes proved to be a formidable weapon in the hands of the Soviet pilots. Their role in the conflict can be summed up by a phrase in which Stalin commented on the first production series aircraft in 1941: "The Sturmovik is as essential to the Red Army as oxygen and bread". In all, more than 35,000 (a record number for the production of combat planes) came off the assembly lines and the construction of the final variants continued until 1955. In fact, after the war, the Il-10 was delivered to the air forces of the satellite countries (Hungary, Rumania, North Korea, Albania, Czechoslovakia, Bulgaria and East Germany), Red China, and after serving in the Korean War, it was withdrawn from the Soviet VVS in 1956.

The origins of the Sturmovik (the Ilyushin fighters were known by this nick-name rather than by their official designations) went back to 1938, when a work team, led by Sergei Vladimorovic Ilyushin, prepared a prototype of a new single-engine ground attack plane and tactical bomber, developed on the basis of official specifications issued by the VVS technical authorities. The aircraft (designated ZKB-55 and characterized by its two-seater structure) appeared in the spring of 1939, and was evaluated immediately. However, the results of the flight tests and initial evaluations were not particularly promising, due above all to the engine's insufficient power and a marked longitudinal instability. It was not until the third prototype, which took to the air on October 12, 1940, that these problems were solved, with the adoption of a more powerful engine, various structural modifications, and the elimination of the observer-gunner position. Officially designated Il-2, the aircraft went into series production immediately, and deliveries to the units commenced at the beginning of April 1941. By the end of June, the VVS had received 249 aircraft which, from their first missions, proved to be formidable weapons against German armored cars and tanks.

The project originality basically lay in having built the aircraft's entire front section (from the engine support to the cockpit) in a single armored shell, which also served a structural function. As well as guaranteeing a maximum protection to the engines and the crew, this solution also allowed for a great weight reduction, compared to a traditional structure that was later fitted with ar-

mor. In addition, the entire fuselage was protected with 4 to 13 mm thick steel plating and 5 mm thick duraluminum. This turned the Il-2 into a veritable "flying tank", making it practically invulnerable to light weapons. This armor was complemented by heavy offensive weaponry which included two 20 mm cannons and up to 1,324 lb (600 kg) of bombs.

In July 1942, the second principal version, the better armed Il-2M3 (also fitted with a more powerful engine, and a second crew member) appeared. This version was produced in the largest quantity. In 1943, efforts to improve the aircraft still further led to the final Il-10 version. Although it retained the basic lay-out of its predecessor, from many points of view, this aircraft represented an entirely new project. It was characterized by an all-metal airframe, remarkable aerodynamic improvements and modifications to the power plant and principal landing gear. The 2,000 hp Mikulin AM-42 engine was adopted; the thickness and extension of its armoring was increase; and its armament received 20 mm and 23 mm cannons. Series production was launched in August 1944, and ceased more than ten years later, after almost 5,000 aircraft had been completed.

color plate
Ilyushin Il-2M3 Soviet Air Force - Oder front, 1945

Aircraft:	Ilyushin Il-10
Nation:	USSR
Manufacturer:	State Industries
Type:	Attack
Year:	1944
Engine:	Mikulin AM-42, 12-cylinder V, liquid-cooled, 2,000 hp
Wingspan:	44 ft 0 in (13.40 m)
Length:	36 ft 4 in (11.06 m)
Height:	11 ft 6 in (3.50 m)
Weight:	13,984 lb (6,335 kg)
Maximum speed:	329 mph (530 km/h) at 7,058 ft (2,400 m)
Ceiling:	13,157 ft (4,000 m)
Range:	496 miles (800 km)
Armament:	2 x 23 mm cannons; 1 x 20 mm cannons; 2 machine guns; 2,207 lb (1,000 kg) of bombs
Crew:	2

A formation of Il-2 assault plane in flight.

FOCKE WULF Fw.190 D-9

In the long evolution of the Focke Wulf Fw.190 while the final Ta.152 (the last project of Kurt Tank in 1937) was being developed, the D variant of 1944 represented a transitional phase. Despite this, from many points of view, the Long-nose Dora (the Fw.190 D became known by this nick-name in the Luftwaffe, due to the lengthening of the front section caused by the installation of the large Junkers Jumo 213A V-12 engine in place of the usual BMW 801 radial) was the most successful version of the entire family. This was mainly due to the engine itself, which was capable of generating no less than 2,240 hp in case of emergency and guaranteed the fighter an excellent performance. The Fw.190 D-12/R21 (one of the numerous subseries developed in the course of production, amounting to a total of almost 700 aircraft) proved to be the fastest of all the Fw.190s, reaching speeds of about 453 mph (730 km/h) at altitude.

Kurt Tank first used an in-line Junkers Jumo engine at the beginning of 1942, when he transformed six Fw.190 A airframes into prototypes. The second phase of evaluations by the Luftwaffe began toward the end of 1943, when some A-7 series aircraft were modified in a similar way to Fw.190 D-0s. Through gradual improvements, the definitive structure was eventually finished and the first Fw.190 D-9 took to the air in May, 1944. Apart from the installation of the in-line engine with a characteristic circular radiator, the most obvious feature of the aircraft was the remarkable lengthening of its fuselage. This together with larger vertical tail planes, made it an aircraft that was noticeably different from its predecessors.

The Fw.190 Ds were initially regarded with suspicion by the Luftwaffe pilots. Eventually, once the crews were familiar with it and the fighter was able to express its true potential, this attitude radically changed. The Dora maintained a remarkable performance, especially in its speed in ascent. It was clearly superior to the aircraft that had radial engines. Its maneuverability and turning radius were also superior. It began its service in September 1944 with the units of the III/JG 54, defending the airports of Hesepe and Achmer, near the Dutch border. It was here that the Nowotny Command, which was evaluating the new Messerschmitt Me.262 jets, was based. Protection was vital, considering that the revolutionary

fighters were particularly vulnerable during takeoff and landing, and the Fw.190 D-9s soon proved to be competitive with the North American P-51D and Supermarine Spitfire Mk.XIVs were concerned. These were two of the Luftwaffe's most feared adversaries.

The Dora equipped many fighter units until the end of the war and several subseries were built, differing from each other mainly in their armament and engines. In addition, numerous experimental versions were studied, most of which would have used new engines, such as the 2,400 hp BMW 802 radials, the 3,900 hp BMW 803 (the latter was a large 28-cylinder engine), and the Daimler Benz DB 609, DB 614 and DB 623. They generated 2,660, 2,020, and 2,400 hp respectively. However, the aircraft's great effectiveness was not very useful during the final, desperate months of the war, when Luftwaffe was hampered by a lack of skilled pilots and a shortage of fuel.

---

color plate

Focke Wulf Fw.190 D-9 II Jagdgeschwader 4, Reichsverteidigung (Defense of the Reich), Luftwaffe - Germany, 1945

Aircraft:	Focke Wulf Fw.190 D-9
Nation:	Germany
Manufacturer:	Focke Wulf Flugzeugbau GmbH
Type:	Fighter-bomber
Year:	1944
Engine:	Junkers Jumo 213A-1, 12-cylinder V, liquid-cooled, 1,700 hp
Wingspan:	34 ft 6 in (10.50 m)
Length:	33 ft 6 in (10.20 m)
Height:	11 ft 0 in (3.35 m)
Weight:	10,684 lb (4,840 kg)
Maximum speed:	425 mph (685 km/h) at 21,710 ft (6,600 m)
Ceiling:	39,473 ft (12,000 m)
Range:	521 mph (840 km/h)
Armament:	2 x 20 mm cannons; 2 machine guns; 1,103 lb (500 kg) of bombs
Crew:	1

A Focke Wulf Fw.190 D-9 with supplementary fuel tank in the belly.

GERMANY

Plagued by incessant bombing raids, forced into defense on all fronts, the Germany of the last two years of the war reacted with a desperate strength, right until the last day, using to the fullest its still highly powerful air force.

1943 saw the powerful Allied war machine working in full force in direct attacks against the Third Reich. In that year no fewer than 135,000 tons of bombs were released on Germany. The missions were planned according to a precise strategy that aimed to reduce the industrial network to chaos and to weaken the population's psychological resistance. 1944 witnessed a further increase in this activity, due in part to the Allied invasion of Europe. In the period between January 1 and June 5, 36 daytime attacks and 102 night raids were carried out, repeatedly involving 37 cities, including Berlin, Braunschweig, Frankfurt-on-Main, Hannover, and Schweinfurt.

In a single week, from February 19 to 25, the RAF and USAAF bomber released 16,700 tons of bombs on German aeronautical factories and airports. Moreover, up till June 1, the bombing raids served above all to prepare the ground for the Allied landings in Normandy, which marked the beginning of the last phase of the conflict in Europe.

In the face of all this, the German reaction was a fierce one. This effort was incredibly sustained by the industrial network, whose potential was stretched to its limits. In mid-1943, fighters alone were produced at a rate of 700 a month, and this number increased still further, to 2,500 aircraft per month, halfway through 1944. In the course of the year, the assembly lines managed to complete the incredible total of 25,500 aircraft of all types. Production peaked in 1944, with 39,800 being constructed.

But this level was remarkable not only from a quantitative point of view. As well as putting a great number of combat planes into production and adapting the principal types already in existence with great flexibility to the changes in operative requirements, the German aeronautical industry also proved capable, in these desperate circumstances, of building entirely new aircraft. These included the remarkable two-engine Heinkel He.219 night fighter (which, right from its operational debut on the night of June 11-12, 1943 proved to be a formidable weapon, one of the best in its category) and the revolutionary Messerschmitt Me.262 and Arado Ar.234 jet planes, which, during their brief career in the final phase of the war, led the Allies to contemplate seriously the still latent potential of their adversary.

Chronology

1943

June. Operative evaluations of the new German Heinkel He.219 *Uhu* night fighter begin. On the night of June 11-12, a preseries aircraft piloted by Major Werner Streib shot down five RAF Lancaster bombers which were heading for Berlin. The He.219 was one of the best aircraft in its category, equal to the outstanding British Mosquito; however, just under 300 were built.

June 15. The prototype of the Arado Ar.234 V-1 Blitz, the world's first jet bomber, takes to the air in Rheine. This aircraft's career began in July 1944, and approximately 200 were built in all.

October 26. The prototype of the Dornier Do.335 V-1 takes to the air. One of the most original combat planes to be built in the course of the entire conflict, it was powered by two engines installed in the nose and the tail, driving a tractor propeller and a thrusting propeller, respectively. The first version, the Do.335 A, appeared toward the end of 1944, but the course of the war interrupted any further development.

1944

March 10. The prototype of the Blohm und Voss BV.238 takes to the air. It was the largest seaplane of the entire war.

December 6. The prototype of the Heinkel He.162 Salamander takes to the air. This small jet interceptor was designed and built in just 90 days and was one of the last aircraft that the Luftwaffe sent into combat. A massive production program was planned, although only 100 or so of these aircraft came off the assembly lines before the war ended and very few of them went into service.

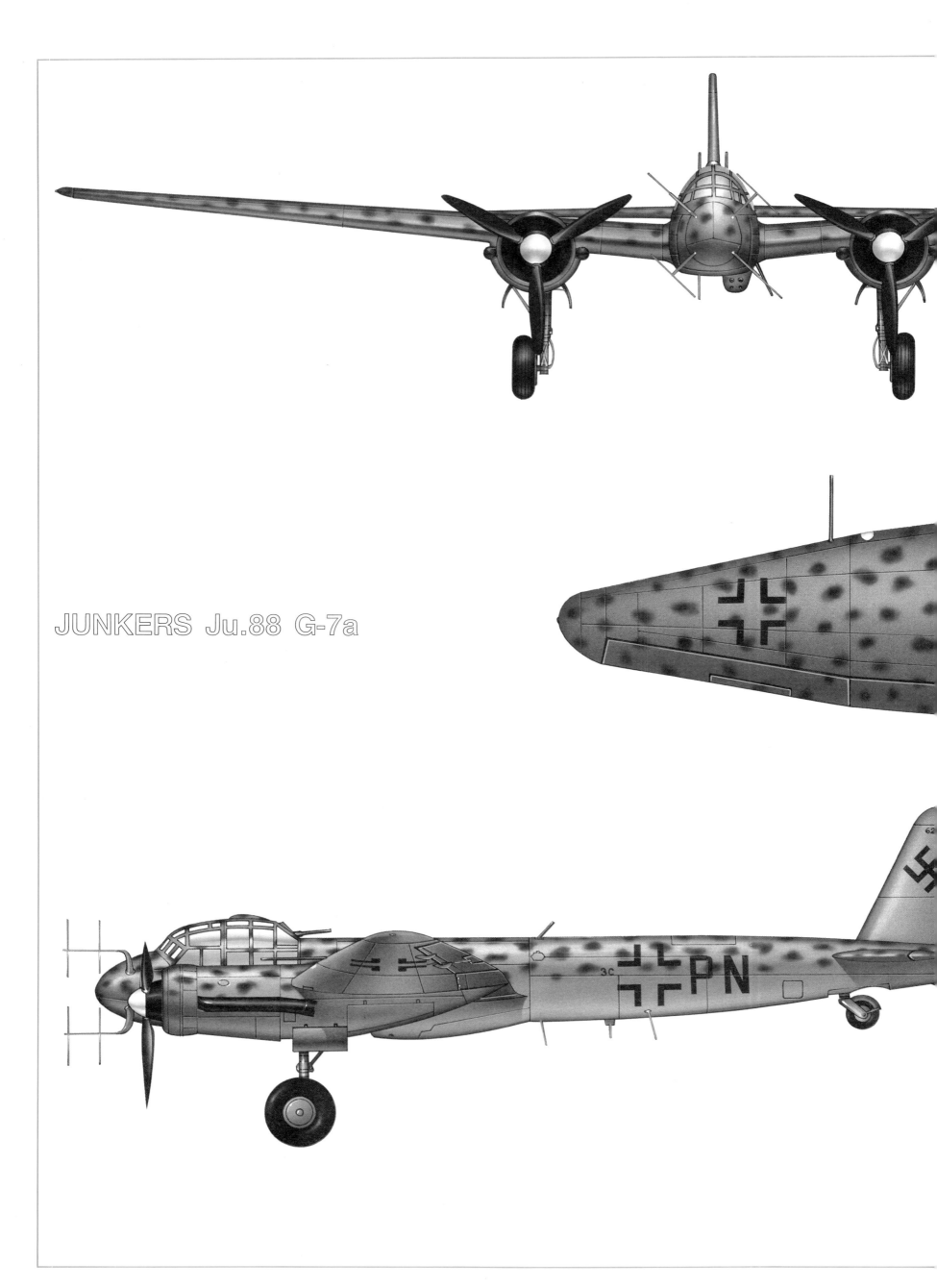

JUNKERS Ju.88 G-7a

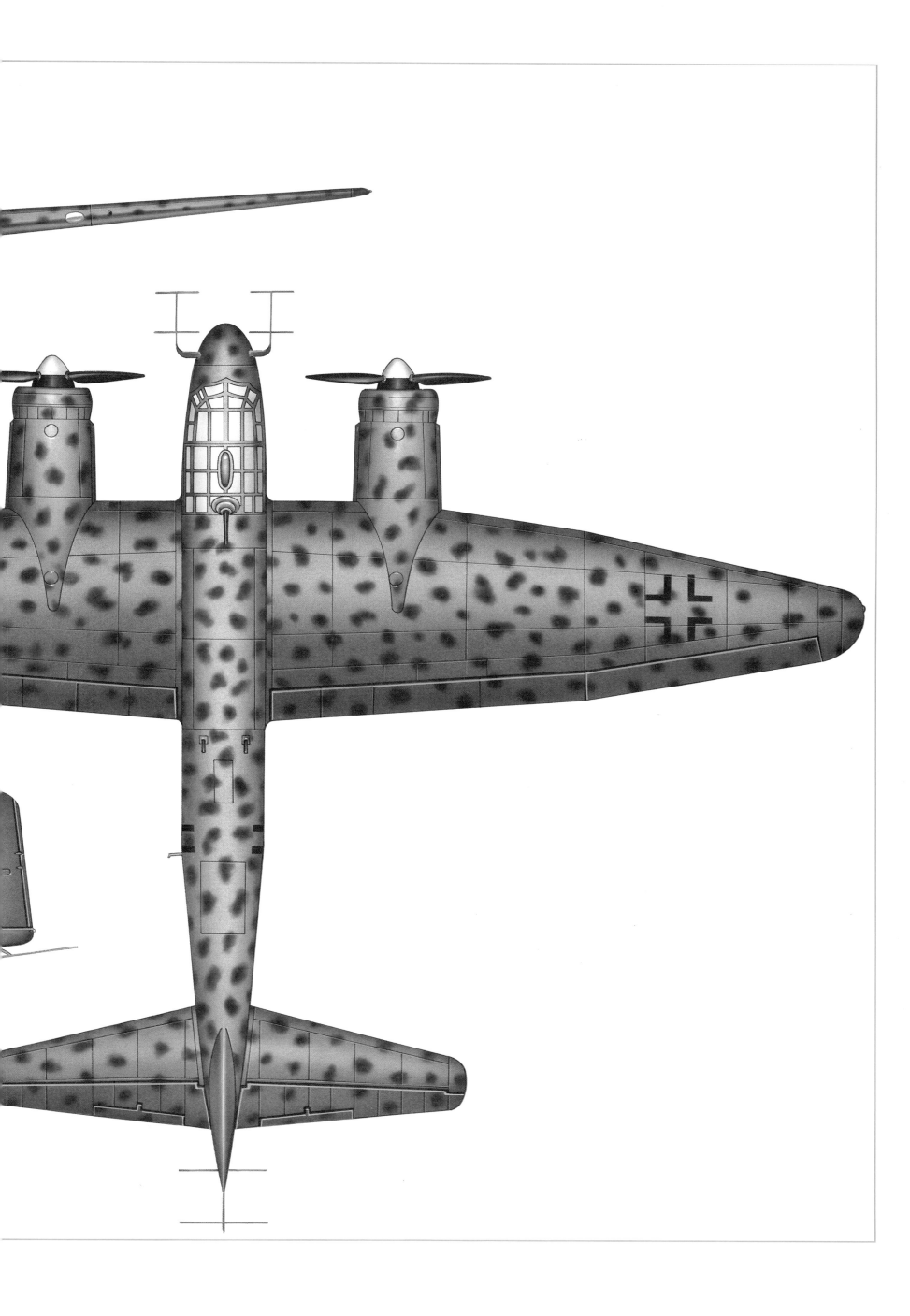

In the long career of the Junkers Ju.88, the night fighter versions held a special importance. Not only because they, perhaps more than any other variant, testified to the great versatility of an aircraft conceived back in 1936 as a fast bomber, but also because in the specific role of night fighters the two-engine Junkers had an intensive and effective operative career, eventually emerging among the best in their category.

The first major production version intended as a night fighter was the Ju.88 C, which went into service in July 1940, in the newly founded *Nachtjagdgeschwader* 1. It was established at the request of Goering himself to oppose the raids carried out by the RAF's Bomber Command. The transformation of the bomber had been carried out on the Ju.88 V-7 prototype. The changes basically consisted of the adoption of a "solid" nose instead of a glazed one, and in the installation of heavy armament in the nose (two 20 mm MG FF cannons and two 7.9 mm MG 17 machine guns). This innovation produced positive results. Although no official request had been made by the Luftwaffe, during 1940, several Ju.88 A-1s were altered in a similar way and they went into production as the Ju.88 C. In addition, 3,200 aircraft were produced in numerous subseries. They differed from each other basically by the type of their radar, the engine, and armament. Mention should be made of the most important of these among which was the Ju.88 C-4 that began production in 1941. This fighter was characterized by an increased wingspan and greater protection. In terms of armament it possessed three 20 mm cannons and three machine guns in the nose.

However, the C series Ju.88s soon proved to be unsuited to their role, weighed down by the large antennae of the radar and the increasingly heavy armament which notably damaged the aircraft's maneuverability at low altitude. In 1943, in order to overcome these limitations, a new prototype was prepared. It adopted the Ju.188's empennages which offered larger surface area, and, in addition, installed a pair of BMW 801 radial engines. This prototype later gave rise to the subsequent G variant.

In the prototype the armament was completely revised. The new features included six 20 mm MG 151 cannons, two installed on the right side of the nose and four in a pod on the left of the belly, and an MG 131 machine gun placed at the second crew member's disposal for the rear defense.

However, in the production series, the two side cannons were removed, and many aircraft retained only those in the belly, with another two similar weapons on their backs.

The latter were installed in a vertical position and slanted in such a way as to fire upward (*Schräge Musik*).

The initial Junkers Ju.88 G-1 variant appeared in the spring of 1944, and was followed by the G-4 (standard avionics), the G-6 (developed in subseries provided both with BMW 801 radials and

A Junkers Ju.88 G-7 with the antennae of the radar apparatus in the nose contained in a conical-shaped wooden fairing.

in-line Jumo 213As), and the final G-7 version, which went into service toward the end of the year. Three subtypes of the latter aircraft (provided with Jumo engines, a water and gas injection system, and larger fuel tanks) were built, and differed basically in their radar systems.

The Junkers Ju.88 Gs proved to be particularly effective in their role and scored notable successes against the formations of enemy bombers. In all, 800 were built before the collapse of the Third Reich.

---

color plate

Junkers Ju.88 G-7a Nachtjagdgeschwader 5 Luftwaffe - Copenhagen-Kastrup, 1945

Aircraft:	Junkers Ju.88 G-7b
Nation:	Germany
Manufacturer:	Junkers Flugzeug und Motorenwerke AG
Type:	Night fighter
Year:	1944
Engine:	2 Junkers Jumo 213E, 12-cylinder V, liquid-cooled, 1,725 hp each
Wingspan:	65 ft 9 in (20.00 m)
Length:	47 ft 9 in (14.53 m)
Height:	15 ft 11 in (4.85 m)
Weight:	28,938 lb (13,109 kg)
Maximum speed:	401 mph (647 km/h) at 29,878 ft (9,083 m)
Ceiling:	32,889 ft (9,997 m)
Range:	1,398 miles (2,252 km)
Armament:	6 x 20 mm cannons; 1 machine gun
Crew:	4

A Junkers Ju.88 G-6 in flight following its capture by the British.

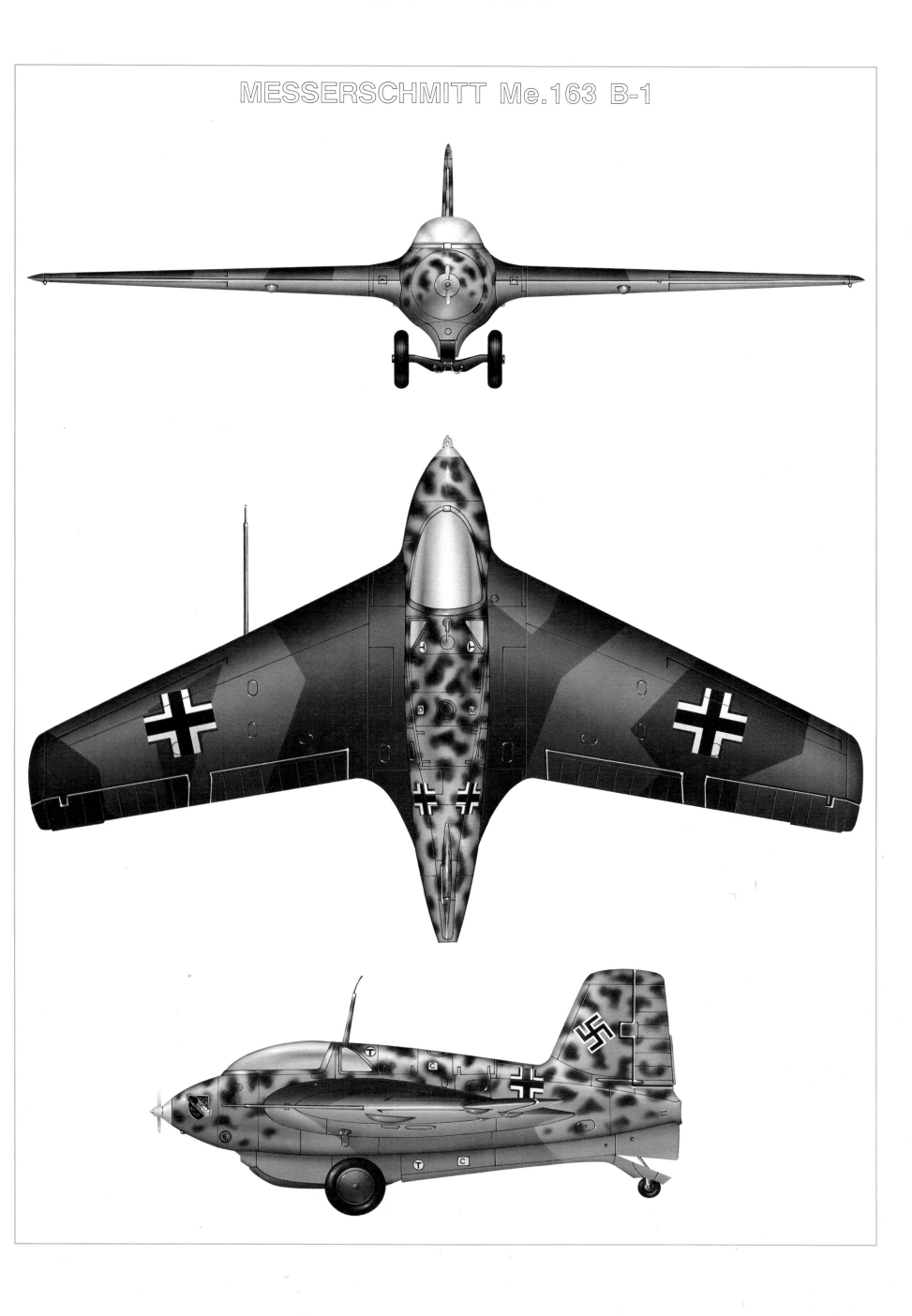

In the forefront of aeronautical production throughout the world, at the time the Messerschmitt Me.163 Komet marked the beginning of a new phase in air warfare. In fact, this revolutionary interceptor was the first aircraft in the world to be powered by a rocket engine, and had it arrived on the scene of the conflict a year earlier, it would certainly have altered the balance between the adversaries. This small and fast combat plane's first mission took place on May 13, 1944. The plane was piloted by Wolfgang Späte over Bad Zwischenahn, the base of the first Luftwaffe unit (the 16th *Erprobungscommando*). This mission, carried out by a preseries aircraft entirely painted in red, came to an end without casualties. It marked the beginning of an intense flying career that was to continue throughout the last year of the war. Nevertheless, the Me.163's career was largely influenced by Germany's critical situation: shortage of fuel, production difficulties due to the continuous and devastating Allied bombing raids, lack of time to prepare the aircraft definitively, and to train the pilots. In all, just over 300 Me.163s were completed before production was interrupted in 1945. Most of these were of the B-1a version (237 aircraft built in 1944, and 42 in January of the following year), the only one to be used in combat.

The Komet was the result of the work of two great aeronautical technicians. The first, Alexander Lippisch, who started to work on the development of all-wing gliders in 1926, developed and perfected the formula, overcoming all problems concerning stability and control. The second, Helmuth Walter, was the designer of the first rocket engine fed by combustible liquids. In fact, the Me.163 was simply a glider which used the revolutionary form of propulsion only for a few moments: the time necessary for takeoff, ascent, attacking, and carrying out escape maneuvers before returning to the ground. Structurally, the aircraft was a small monoplane, built of several materials; the pilot, rocket engine, and fuel were installed in the fuselage, and the armament was located on the half-wing root.

The project was launched at the beginning of 1939, when Lippisch and his work team started to collaborate in great secrecy with the Messerschmitt company in Augsburg. Work went ahead very slowly and the first prototype without an engine was tested at the beginning of 1941. It was towed and then released at altitude by a two engine Messerschmitt Bf.110.

On August 13, Heini Dittmar, the chief test pilot, carried out the first flight with an engine, and on October 2 for the first time ever, he reached Mach 0.84: the recorded speed was 623.4 mph (1,003.9 km/h), about 155 mph (250 km/h) above the official world record. The tests continued, above all to perfect the takeoff procedure (carried out by means of an unhookable under-carriage, while landing took place on a belly skid) and the functioning of the propellers, which were extremely delicate and unstable. This

An Me.163 B that was captured and tested by the British.

process was not without problems, and many disasters clouded the long cycle of preparations.

Following the construction of ten preseries Me.163 A-0s, the Me.163 B prototype took to the air on February 21, 1943, while deliveries of the first aircraft of the initial production series, the Me.163 B-1a, began in May 1944. The first encounter with the Allied bombers took place on July 28, near Merseburg.

Five Komets of the 1/JG 400 attacked a formation of American B-17s. However, their combat activity threw light on a series of defects: firing difficulties, caused by the high speed at which the Me.163s approached the bombers (making it possible only to fire in 3 seconds); problems with controlling the engine (which had a duration of seven and a half minutes) that could only be turned off. Production of the Me.163 B-1 ceased in February 1945, before the aircraft could be tuned definitively. Other projects included the Me.163 C-1a version (three of which were built), with a modified airframe and engine to increase the duration of the thrust and the Me.163 D, provided with retractable forward tricycle landing gear and further improvements. Only one prototype was built which, in the end, was redesignated Me.263.

color plate
Messerschmitt Me.163 B-1 2nd Staffel Jagdgeschwader 400 Luftwaffe - Germany, 1944-1945

Aircraft:	Messerschmitt Me.163 B-1a
Nation:	Germany
Manufacturer:	Messerschmitt AG
Type:	Fighter
Year:	1944
Engine:	Walter HWK 509 A-2 (rocket)
Potency:	3,752 lb (1,700 kg)
Wingspan:	30 ft 7 in (9.32 m)
Length:	19 ft 3 in (5.84 m)
Height:	9 ft 1 in (2.77 m)
Weight:	9,072 lb (4,110 kg)
Maximum speed:	596 mph (960 km/h) at 9,868 ft (3,000 m)
Ceiling:	39,802 ft (12,100 m)
Range:	80 miles (130 km)
Armament:	2 x 30 mm cannons
Crew:	1

The Me.163 seen from the front with the landing gear that was released after take-off.

SUPERMARINE SPITFIRE Mk.XIV

DW D   RB159

Following the experiences with the initial versions of the Rolls-Royce Griffon engine (which had led to the construction of the Spitfire Mk.XII in 1943), the second phase in the career of Reginald J. Mitchell's immortal fighter proceeded rapidly, developing alongside the evolution of the engine. The new variant, the Mk.XIV became the most important in the last year of the conflict. 957 aircraft came off the assembly lines before making way for the "definitive" version with the Griffon engine, the Mk.XVIII, which went into service once the war was over.

The Spitfire Mk.XIIs went into service in the spring of 1943, and their career was marked by notable successes. Their performance was remarkable as far as horizontal speed was concerned, reaching 368 mph (593 km/h) at sea level, compared to the Spitfire Mk.IX's 311 mph (502 km/h). In fact, it was these outstanding results, together with the availability of a stronger and improved versions of the power plant, that led to the creation of the new variant.

The Mk.XIVs were also transitional aircraft. In fact, the prototypes of these aircraft were obtained by modifying six Mk.VIIIs taken directly from the assembly lines. Apart from the installation of a Rolls-Royce Griffon 65 fitted with a two-stage two-speed supercharger (capable of generating more than 2,050 hp and controlling a five-bladed propeller) the basic differences lay in the aircraft's general reinforcement and in the enlargement of the tail planes' surface area.

Deliveries of the first production series aircraft began in October 1943. After an intensive series of tests, the first unit to receive the

401st Squadron, shot down the first Messerschmitt Me.262 of the war.

The evolution of the aircraft proceeded without interruption, although the final variants of the Spitfire were not ready in time to be used in combat. The subsequent series was the Mk.XVIII (300 of which were completed), which was basically redesigned, fitted with reinforced wings and landing gear, and provided with larger fuel tanks and a drop canopy. The power plant was a 2,375 hp Griffon 67.

Some 225 Spitfire Mk.XIXs were built exclusively for use as high altitude photoreconnaissance planes. They lacked armament and were provided with a pressurized cockpit. The original airframe reached its final development in these variants and the three subsequent models built immediately after the war (F.21, F.22, and F.24) were subjected to substantial restructuring, especially in regard to the wings, tail planes, and landing gear. With the production of these aircraft, the total number of Spitfires with Griffon engines delivered to the Royal Air Force reached 2,053. The aircraft's last flight in a front-line unit took place on April 1, 1954, carried out by a PR 19 in service with the 81st Squadron. This was approximately 18 years and one month after the original prototype had made its maiden flight.

color plate

Supermarine Spitfire Mk.XIV 610th Fighter Squadron Royal Air Force - England, 1944. Personal plane of Squadron Leader R.A. Newbury, Commanding officer of the Squadron

Aircraft:	Supermarine Spitfire Mk.XIV
Nation:	Great Britain
Manufacturer:	Supermarine Division of Vickers-Armstrong Ltd.
Type:	Fighter
Year:	1944
Engine:	Rolls-Royce Griffon 65, 12-cylinder V, liquid-cooled, 2,078 hp
Wingspan:	36 ft 10 in (11.22 m)
Length:	32 ft 8 in (9.95 m)
Height:	12 ft 8 in (3.87 m)
Weight:	8,509 lb (3,855 kg)
Maximum speed:	450 mph (724 km/h) at 26,069 ft (7,925 m)
Ceiling:	44,615 ft (13,563 m)
Range:	459 miles (740 km)
Armament:	2 x 20 mm cannons; 4 machine guns; 500 lb (227 kg) of bombs
Crew:	1

A Spitfire Mk.XIV with canopy linked to the fuselage.

new Spitfires was the RAF's 610th Squadron in January of the following year.

The Mk.XIVs of the initial production lot had wings with two 20 mm cannons, four 7.7 mm machine guns and a support for a 500 lb (227 kg) bomb. Subsequently, however, an "E" type universal wing was adopted, with standard armament consisting of two 12.7 mm machine guns, two 20 mm cannons and up to 1,002 lb (454 kg) of bombs. Two subseries were built by the assembly lines: the first in a fighter structure (527 built) and the second for low altitude photoreconnaissance (FR Mk.XIV, of which 430 were built). Both could be fitted with F or LF wings, depending upon the type of mission to be carried out. The final production series aircraft were fitted with a drop canopy, instead of the traditional kind.

The Mk.XIVs' great qualities of speed proved valuable not only in opposing the latest German fighters (also those with rocket engines), but also the threat posed by the V-1 flying bombs. During the last phase of the conflict in Europe, these Spitfires succeeded in destroying no less than 300 of these deadly German weapons.

Moreover, on October 5, 1944, a Mk.XIV, in service with the

The prototype of the Spitfire Mk.XIV, built using the airframe of the Spitfire Mk.VIII.

GREAT BRITAIN

The year 1943 saw the powerful Allied war machine working at full power. On the European front, this led to the British and Americans being directly involved in the attack against Germany. In fact, this was the year in which the two allies established a division of tasks which was to remain practically unaltered until the end of the conflict. The RAF assumed responsibility for the massive night raids, bombing particular areas and using substantially incendiary bombs. The USAAF, on the other hand, was entrusted with the daytime missions (which had been limited in the course of 1942) against individual targets. The alternation became increasingly frequent, and these missions eventually became continuous. The first uninterrupted raid took place on July 24-25 on Hamburg, with the British carrying out a night raid, followed by an American attack the next day. In addition, the targets were clearly defined, according to a precise strategic plan. In the first three months, the missions were directed mainly against submarine bases and shipyards. Later on, the attacks were primarily aimed at the aeronautical industry, as well as factories which produced the relative components for them. Lastly, at the end of the year, the raids on Berlin began.

During 1943, no fewer than 135,000 tons of bombs were released on Germany. Among the heaviest raids, those on Hamburg (11,000 tons), Essen (9,000 tons) and Cologne (8,000 tons) should be remembered for their devastating effects. In particular, it has been estimated that, in 1943, the Allied bombings caused a 10 percent reduction in the total German production.

The following year, this activity was increased still further, and from February 1944, the new "double blow" technique was adopted for the first time. This consisted of a raid being repeated on the same target, within a brief space of time. In the period between January 1 and June 5, 36 daytime raids and 102 night-time raids were carried out, involving 37 cities, including Berlin (17 bombing raids), Braunschweig (13), Frankfurt-on-Main (8), Hannover, and Schweinfurt (5 raids). In one week alone, from February 19 to 25, the RAF and USAAF bombers released 16,700 tons of bombs on German aeronautical factories and airports. Moreover, until June 1, the bombing missions were rigorously planned to prepare the ground for the Normandy landings which, for their part, marked the beginning of the last, bloody phase of the war in Europe.

This huge effort, costly in terms both of men and aircraft, saw the British aircraft industry engaged to its full, limits reaching new qualitative and quantitative levels. In 1944, total production amounted to 29,220 aircraft of all types, compared to the 26,263 produced in 1943, 23,761 in 1942, 20,100 in 1941, 15,000 in 1940, and 7,000 in 1939.

Chronology

1943

January. The Fairey Barracuda begins its career. This was the first carried-based torpedo monoplane constructed in Great Britain. This aircraft, of which 2,572 were built, distinguished itself in all the air-sea operations of the last two years of the war.

February. The first Supermarine Spitfire Mk.XII with Rolls-Royce Griffon engine is delivered to the RAF's 41st Squadron, based at Hawkinge, in Kent. These aircraft, which became operative in the spring, gave rise to the second generation of Spitfires and were put into service to oppose the threat of the German Focke Wulf Fw.190 raiders along the southern coasts of Britain.

March 5. The fifth prototype of the Gloster Meteor fighter takes to the air for the first time. This was the only Allied combat plane powered by jet engines to be used in the conflict. The Meteor never managed to defeat its direct rival, the Messerschmitt Me.262.

June 21. The first production series Hawker Tempest Mk.V, the best single-seater built by Hawker during the conflict, takes to the air. It went into service in April 1944, and thanks to its remarkable speed and its powerful armament, it proved to be a formidable weapon in the interception of the German V-1 flying bombs.

September 20. The prototype of the de Havilland Vampire, the second British jet fighter, takes to the air. This aircraft did not succeed in entering front-line service during the conflict, although it had a long and intensive career after the war.

October 1. The first Fairey Firefly carrier-based fighters go into service, on board the aircraft carrier *Indefatigable*. This strong and powerful two-seater had its baptism of fire in July of the following year, in Norway, during operations against the German battleship *Tirpitz*.

1944

June 9. The first prototype of the Avro Lincoln takes to the air. The Lincoln was the natural result of the formula which had led to the Lancaster's creation. This aircraft did not go into service until the war was practically over. A total of 582 were built. It remained in service in the units of Bomber Command until the end of 1955.

July 27. The new Gloster Meteor jet fighters carry out their first combat missions against the German V-1 flying bombs. The first of these bombs was shot down on August 4. In all, the Meteors succeeded in destroying 13 bombs before the end of the war.

July 28. The prototype of the de Havilland Hornet, the RAF's last fighter with a piston engine, takes to the air. Derived from the famous Mosquito, it did not take part in World War II. In all, 391 were built, equipping the units of the RAF and the Fleet Air Arm.

December 4. The prototype of the Bristol Brigand attack plane takes to the air. Conceived as the Beaufighter's successor, this aircraft arrived too late to participate actively in the conflict and remained in front-line service well into the second half of the 1950s.

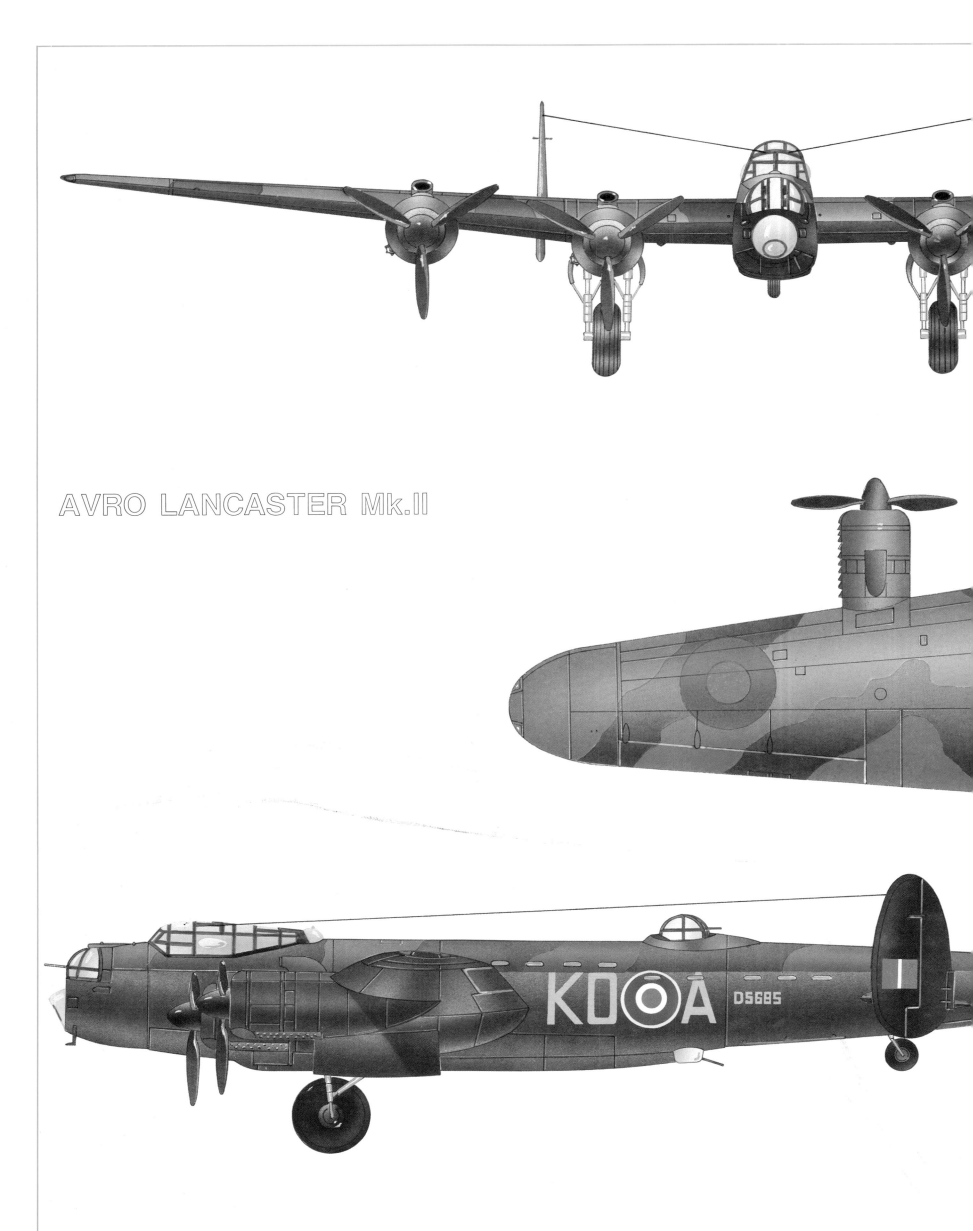

AVRO LANCASTER Mk.II

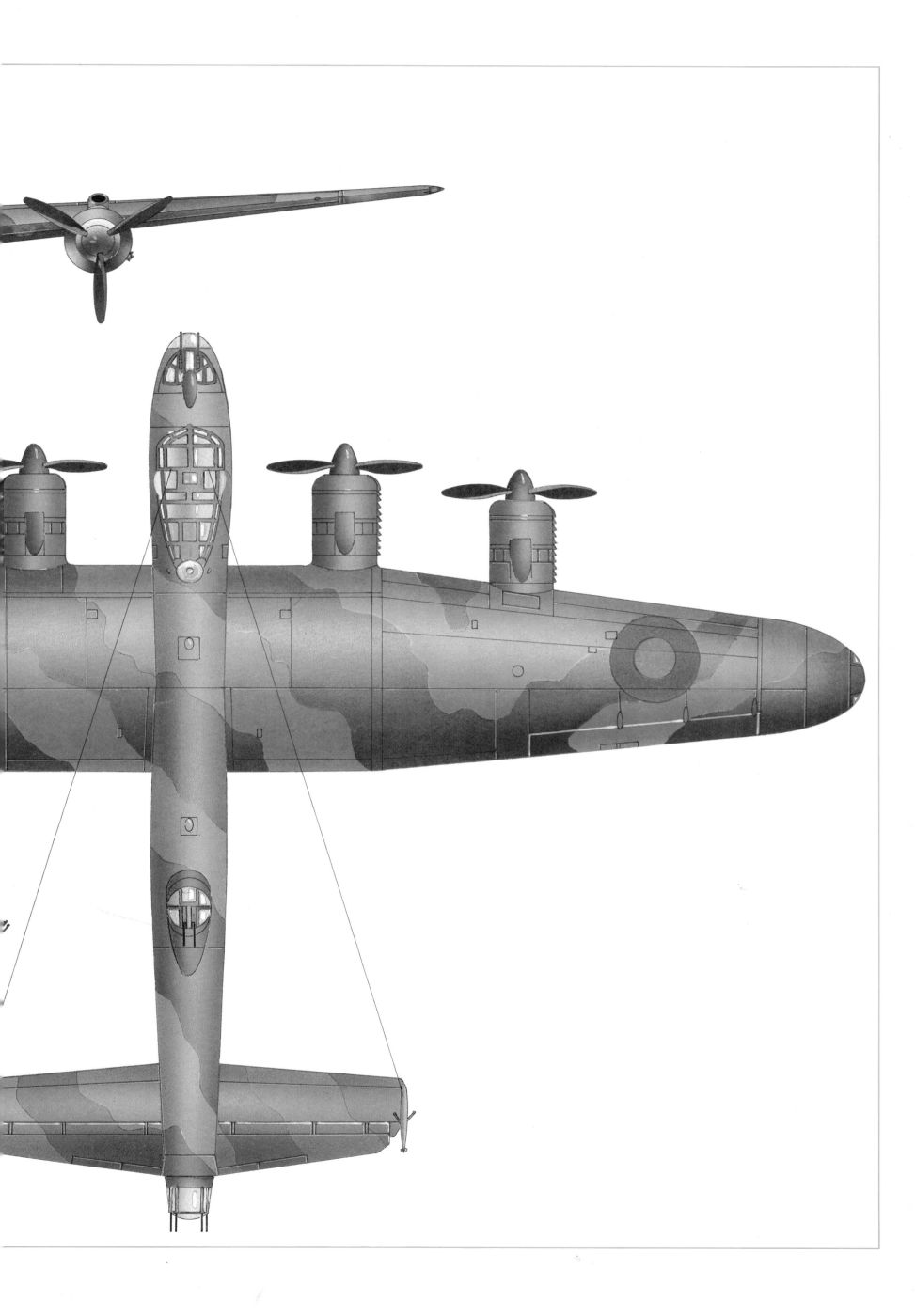

The Lancaster's great success and the high production rate that had been imposed back in 1941, soon created a shortage of Rolls-Royce Merlin engines. In fact, this prestigious engine equipped practically all of the most successful aircraft built by the British aeronautical industry (from the Spitfire to the Hurricane, from the Mosquito to the numerous types of aircraft in the Fleet Air Arm, as well as the Lancaster itself) and its assembly lines went ahead at full speed in order to satisfy the increasing demand. It was therefore the actual need to compensate for possible deficiency in the supply of the engine that led to the construction of a second production variant of the bomber, fitted with an alternative engine. The 1,735 hp Bristol Hercules radial (the VI and XVI versions) was selected and installed on a Lancaster prototype in the second half of 1941.

The aircraft was flown for the first time on November 26, and at the beginning of the following year, together with another two experimental aircraft, it was submitted to an intensive cycle of evaluations. The results were satisfactory, and production was launched immediately afterwards, with the designation Lancaster Mk.II. The new bombers went into service in March 1943, and they gradually began to re-equip several units of Bomber Command.

However, despite its good overall characteristics, the Lancaster Mk.II never succeeded in equaling those fitted with Merlin engines. Although its performance in takeoff, ascent and at low altitude was better, it was slower in flight and consumed more fuel. Production ceased after 301 had been completed. The decision to abandon the radial engines also occurred due to the arrival in Great Britain of the first Rolls-Royce Merlin engines built in the United States by Packard. This new and plentiful supply eventually dispelled all fears of a shortage of these plants.

The subsequent Mk.III version was in fact fitted with American engines, and, apart from this and slight modifications to the tip of the nose, it was practically identical to the first production variant. A total of 3,039 were built in all. The final version was designated Mk.VII (180 built). The American Martin turret on the aircraft's back was its only major difference. Moreover, 430 Lancasters were built in Canada by the Victory Aircraft company and designated Mk.X. They were fitted with Packard-Merlin engines. The first was completed on August 6, 1943.

Lastly, mention should be made of a special subseries (very few were built) created by the conversion of several Lancaster Mk.Is and Mk.IIIs. This was the Mk.VII, which appeared toward the end of 1944, and was characterized by Merlin engines generating 1,635 hp and each controlling four-bladed propeller instead of a three-bladed one. These aircraft, which lacked armament, apart from the turret on their back, carried electronic ap-

A line up of Lansters at Waterbeach, in 1944.

paratus, thus creating disturbance in the enemy's radar.

The end of the war did not mark the end of the Lancaster's career. These four-engine aircraft remained in front-line service with Bomber Command for a long period, until the arrival of the Avro Lincoln immediately after the war. Many were subsequently modified for photoreconnaissance and remained in service until the 1950s.

---

color plate

Avro Lancaster Mk.II 115th Squadron Royal Air Force. This aircraft was shot down on the night of August 2-3, 1944, during a raid on Hamburg

---

Aircraft:	Avro Lancaster Mk.II
Nation:	Great Britain
Manufacturer:	A.V. Roe & Co. Ltd.
Type:	Bomber
Year:	1943
Engine:	4 Bristol Hercules VI, 14-cylinder radial, air-cooled, 1,735 hp each
Wingspan:	102 ft 3 in (31.09 m)
Length:	69 ft 8 in (21.18 m)
Height:	20 ft (6.10 m)
Weight:	63,083 lb (28,577 kg)
Maximum speed:	264 mph (426 km/h) at 14,036 ft (4,267 m)
Ceiling:	18,552 ft (5,640 m)
Range:	2,547 miles (4,103 km)
Armament:	10 machine guns; 14,017 lb (6,350 kg) of bombs
Crew:	7

A Lancaster flying with only one engine working.

This Lancaster is one of the thirty aircraft shot down during the raid against Hamburg.

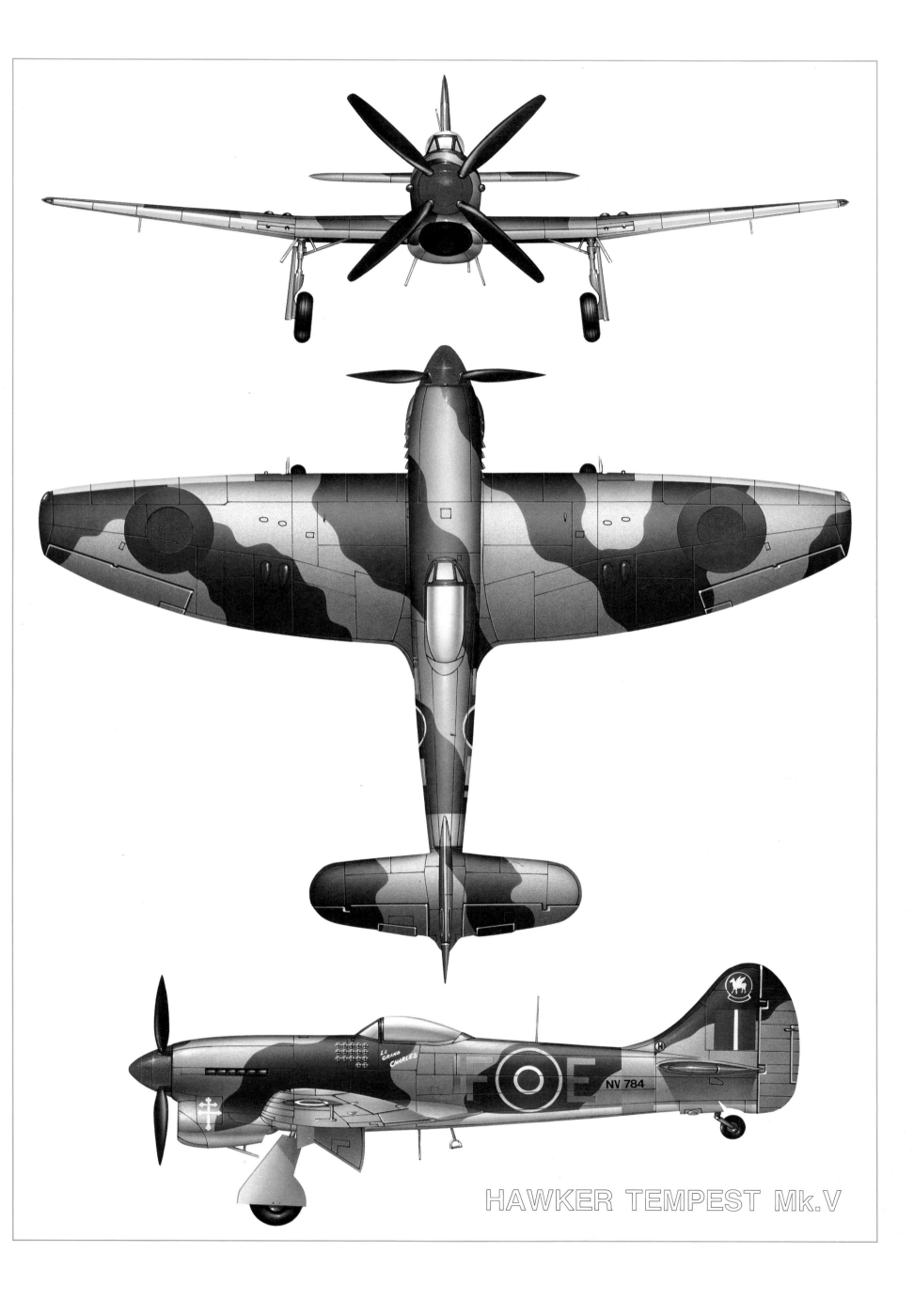

HAWKER TEMPEST Mk.V

In 1940, the Hawker Tempest represented the optimal development of the project which had given rise to the Typhoon, an aircraft that had proved to be disappointing as an interceptor, although formidable as an attack plane. Among the fastest of the propeller-driven combat planes sent into action by the RAF during the last year of the war, the Tempest distinguished itself in two particular tasks (also true of the Spitfire Mk.XIV): the pursuit of German V-1 flying bombs and the interception of the Luftwaffe's revolutionary Me.262 jet. The principal production variant during the war was the Mk.V. Up till August 1945 800 were built. The Tempest Mk.VI (142 built, differed mainly in the adoption of a 2,300 hp Napier Sabre engine) and those of the Mk.II series (764 of these were built, differing radically in that they were fitted with a 2,526 hp Bristol Centaurus radial engine) were not ready in time to participate in the war. Nevertheless, the last Tempests remained in service until 1949 and 1951, respectively.

Sydney Camm, the Hawker's chief designer, had set to work on the new project at the time of the Typhoon's first tests, with the aim of improving it. The modifications were concentrated above all on the wing, whose structure, profile and shape were completely redesigned. Different engines were chosen for the new fighter (originally designated Typhoon Mk.II, and subsequently rechristened Tempest): the 24-cylinder Napier Sabre for the Mk.I and Mk.V series; the "V-12" Rolls-Royce Griffon for the Mk.III series; and the 18-cylinder Bristol Centaurus for the Mk.II series. After the Tempest Mk.I remained at the prototype stage and following the abandonment of the project powered by the Rolls-Royce Griffon, the only basic variants that eventually went into production were the Mk.V, fitted with a Napier Sabre engine, and the Mk.II, with the Centaurus radial.

The first prototype of the family to take to the air was the Mk.V, on September 2, 1942, and the first production series aircraft appeared on June 21 of the following year. This aircraft went into service in April 1944, and right from its first missions it proved to have an outstanding performance, not only interception and altitude combat, but also in ground attack. The Tempest Mk.V was much faster than almost all its adversaries and many of its Allied counterparts. This characteristic immediately rendered it indispensible in facing the threat posed by the German V-1 flying bombs.

Its success in this particular role can be seen with the aid of a few figures. From June 13 to September 5, 1944, the merit for no fewer than 638 of the 1,771 V-1s destroyed by the British air defense was due to the Tempests. A precise combat tactic was prepared. Provided with supplementary fuel tanks that permitted

A Tempest Mk.V in flight with supplementary fuel tanks below the wings.

A Tempest Mk.II with Bristol Centaurus radial engine.

a maximum of four and a half hours patrolling time, the fighters flew at 9,868 ft (3,000 m), maintaining constant contact with the radar stations on the ground, which quickly supplied them with details of the paths of the V-1s. The attack was generally carried out during a dive, in that the bombs flew at altitudes ranging from 986 ft (300 m) to 7,894 ft (2,400 m), allowing the Tempests to acquire notable advantages in speed. The heavy armament on board did the rest. Although in some cases, once the ammunition was finished, many pilots succeeded in arriving alongside the V-1s and making them plunge into the sea by tipping them over with the tips of their wings.

As for the Tempest Mk.II, this prototype took to the air for the first time on June 28, 1943, and the first production series aircraft was completed on October 4 of the following year. The prototype of the Mk.VI version made its maiden flight on May 9, 1944.

A Hawker Tempest pictured at the time of the Normandy landings with invasion stripes.

color plate

Hawker Tempest Mk.V 3rd Squadron Royal Air Force - Belgium 1944. Personal aircraft of Wing Commander Pierre Clostermann

Aircraft:	Hawker Tempest Mk.V
Nation:	Great Britain
Manufacturer:	Hawker Aircraft Co. Ltd.
Type:	Fighter-bomber
Year:	1944
Engine:	Napier Sabre 11A, 24-cylinder H, liquid-cooled, 2,210 hp
Wingspan:	41 ft 1 in (12.50 m)
Length:	33 ft 9 in (10.26 m)
Height:	16 ft 1 in (4.90 m)
Weight:	13,558 lb (6,142 kg)
Maximum speed:	435 mph (702 km/h) at 18,552 (5,640 m)
Ceiling:	36,595 ft (11,125 m)
Range:	738 miles (1,190 km)
Armament:	4 x 20 mm cannons; 2,004 lb (908 kg) of bombs
Crew:	1

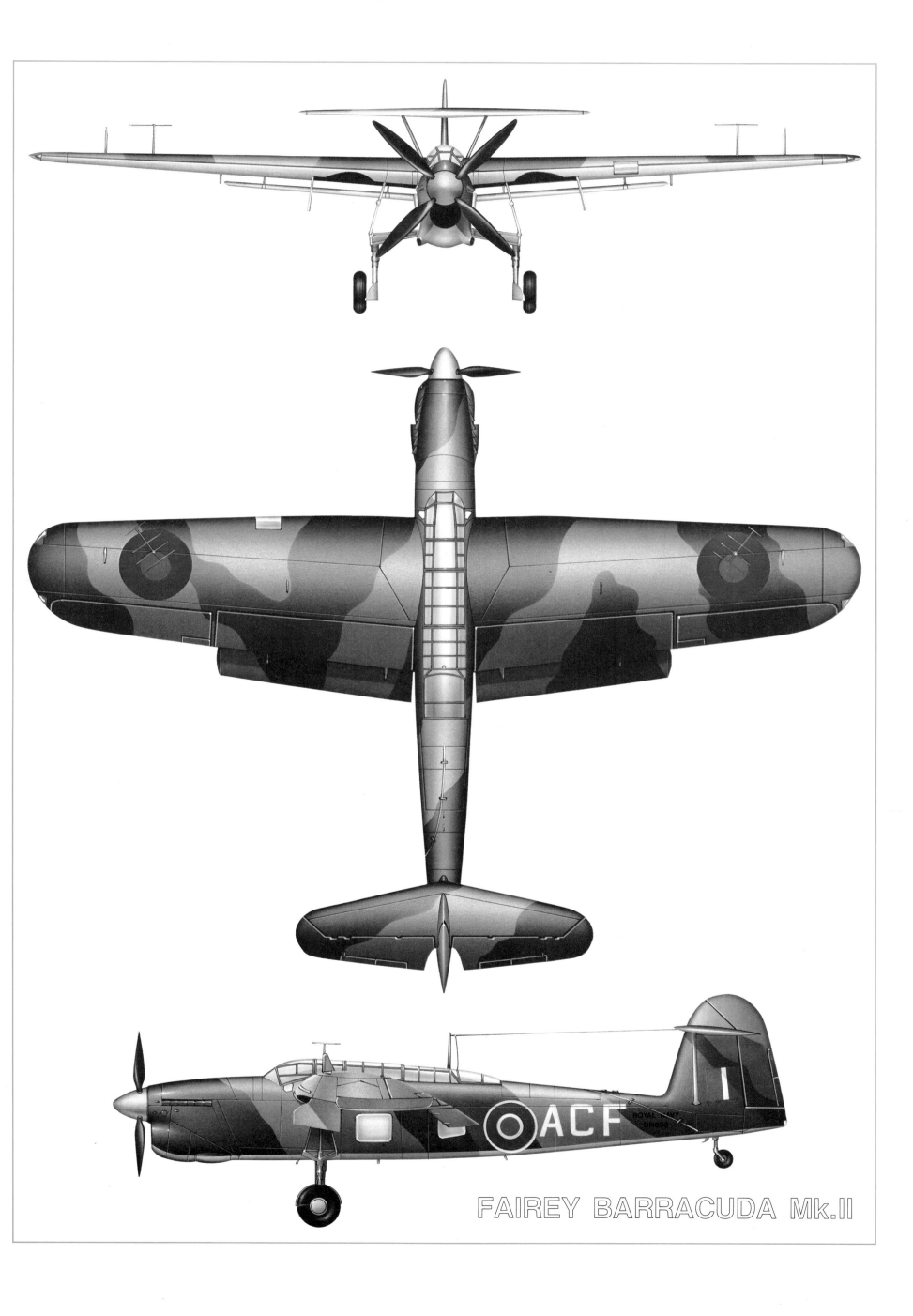

FAIREY BARRACUDA Mk.II

Considered one of the British Fleet Air Arm's most versatile combat planes during the last years of the war, the Fairey Barracuda was also the first all-metal carrier-based monoplane torpedo plane to be built in Great Britain. These aircraft, used as torpedo planes, bombers, and dive-bombers, went into front-line service early in 1943, ant took part in all subsequent air-sea operations. Many of the approximately 2,600 Barracudas survived the war and remained in active service until 1953, when they were replaced by the American Grumman Avengeres.

The project was launched back in 1937, on the basis of specifications issued by the British Air Ministry that called for the construction of a carrier-based torpedo plane to replace the Albacore biplanes. Six companies participated and eventually, in July 1938, Fairey obtained an order for two prototypes. Initially the choice of engine fell on the new Rolls-Royce Exe (24-cylinders, generating 1,207 hp), but when the program for its development was abandoned, it was decided to install a Merlin 30 engine in the Mk.I production version. The first prototype made its maiden flight on December 7, 1940, and was followed by the second experimental aircraft on June 29, 1941. The aircraft was an all-metal mid-cantilever wing three-seater monoplane, fitted with Fairey-Youngman high lifting devices which remarkably improved its performance at low speed. The cycle of evaluation tests was not completed until February 1942. Production, soon after, went ahead at full speed.

However, only 30 Barracuda Mk.Is came off the assembly lines before the second Mk.II variant was prepared. This differed mainly in its more powerful engine. In order to face the substantial demand, other aeronautical companies were called upon to participate in the program. These included Blackburn, Boulton Paul and Westland. A total of 1,688 aircraft were built.

The Barracuda Mk.II went into service in January 1943, with the 827th Squadron, although it did not receive its baptism of fire until eight months later, in September, during the Allied landings at Salerno. This aircraft's most memorable endeavour took place on April 3, 1944, off the northern coast of Norway, when 42 Barracudas stationed on the aircraft carriers *Victorious* and *Furious* (escorted by Hellcat, Seafire, Wildcat and Corsair fighters) attacked in two waves the German battleship *Tirpitz*, which had taken shelter in a fjord. They inflicted damage that was not irreparable, but which seriously diminished the vessel's capacities. Similar missions were

carried out in the next four months, until the *Tirpitz* was eventually sunk by Lancaster bombers on November 12. In April 1944, the Barracudas also appeared in the Pacific, operating from on board the aircraft carrier *Illustrious*.

The next production variant, the Mk.III, was developed in 1943, expressly for antishipping and anti-submarine attacks. With this aim in mind, radar research apparatus was installed in a radome beneath the rear section of the fuselage. The Barracuda Mk.III went into production in 1944, and 852 were completed.

The last version of the series was the Mk.V, characterized by the adoption of a 2,058 hp Rolls-Royce Griffon 37 engine and by consequent structural modifications (greater wingspan, increase in fuel capacity, and tail fins with a larger surface area). However, its development was very slow, and the first production series aircraft did not appear until November 16, 1944. Of the 140 aircraft ordered, only 30 were delivered before the end of the war. These aircraft never went into service and served as trainers until 1950.

---

color plate
Fairey Barracuda Mk.II 715th Squadron Royal Navy Air Service - Yeovilton/St. Merryn, 1943-1944

Aircraft:	Fairey Barracuda Mk.II
Nation:	Great Britain
Manufacturer:	Fairey Aviation Co. Ltd.
Type:	Torpedo plane
Year:	1943
Engine:	Rolls-Royce Merlin 32, 12-cylinder V, liquid-cooled, 1,663 hp
Wingspan:	49 ft 3 in (14.99 m)
Length:	39 ft 10 in (12.12 m)
Height:	15 ft 1 in (4.60 m)
Weight:	14,119 lb (6,396 kg)
Maximum speed:	240 mph (386 km/h) at 1,809 ft (550 m)
Ceiling:	16,447 ft (5,000 m)
Range:	683 miles (1,100 km)
Armament:	2 machine guns; 1,642 lb (744 kg) of bombs
Crew:	3

A Fairey Barracuda Mk.II in flight.

THE BOMBING RAIDS ON GERMANY

The night of May 16-17, 1943. Eighteen Avro Lancaster bombers from the RAF's 617th Squadron destroy the dams on the Möhne and Eder rivers, in the very heart of the Ruhr, which supplied 75 percent of the electricity to the factories of the valley. The Lancasters had been purposely modified to carry and release special "rolling bombs" prepared by Barnes Wallis, designer at Vickers. The raid, which resulted in the loss of eight aircraft and 55 men, was led by Wing Commander Guy Gibson, and, apart from its effects, it has gone down in history as one of the most daring and sensational attempts to violate German territory, and, perhaps, as the very example of the thousands of raids which, in the second half of the conflict in Europe, the Allies carried out incessantly against their main direct adversary.

This new phase of the war in the air began almost immediately after the Battle of Britain. In 1941, the bombing missions against the Third Reich acquired increasing weight and importance. From July onward, RAF's Bomber Command was entrusted with the task not only of attacking industrial targets, but also of damaging the German communications network and weakening the morale of the population, above all that in the industrialized areas of the Ruhr and the Rheine valley. The first carpet bombing raids were carried out, with great employment of incendiary bombs. Although the concrete results were not particularly great, much effort was expended: in the course of the year, the amount of bombs released on enemy territory reached 35,000 tons.

In 1942, a decisive boost was received, with the arrival in Great Britain of the first American units of the 8th USAAF, which gradually operated alongside those of the RAF. The greater number of aircraft available decidedly increased the strategic value of these missions. From March onward, bombing techniques were also modified. The waves of aircraft were replaced by massive concentrations on a single target. The first raid of this type took place on the night of March 28-29 on Lubeck, involving almost 300 bombers which released 500 tons of bombs on the city. Similar missions followed on Rostock, and on the night of May 30, the first "1,000 aircraft" raid took place on Cologne. On June 1-2, a mission of this type was repeated on Essen, and on June 25-26, on Bremen.

These experiences, among other things, led to further improvements in the techniques of location of targets and also those related to the coordination of enormous numbers of aircraft. The results proved to be devastating. During the year 1942, the territory of the Third Reich was subjected to 1,000 raids, 17 of which were on a large scale with more than 500 tons of bombs being released.

1943 witnessed the powerful Allied war machine working to its full potential. In fact, in that year, the British and Americans established a division of tasks that was to remain practically unaltered until the end of the war. The RAF assumed responsibility for the massive night raids, with bombings of limited areas and the wide employment of incendiary bombs. The USAAF, on the other hand, assumed responsibility for the daytime missions (which had been limited in the course of 1942) against individual targets. On January 27, the 8th USAAF carried out its first raid on Germany, using 53 aircraft in the Wilhelmshaven area, and a small diversionary force on Emden. On June 22, it carried out its first massive daytime attack on the Ruhr, using 182 bombers. This alternation between the British and the Americans became increasingly frequent until the raids became practically continuous. The first uninterrupted raid took place on July 24-25 on Hamburg, with the British bombing at night, and the Americans, the following day. In addition, the targets were clearly defined, following a precise strategic plan. During the first three months, the raids were directed mainly against submarine bases and shipyards; subsequently they were aimed above all at the aeronautical industry and those which produced related components. Of the many missions, mention should be made of the one carried out on August 17 by 315 B-17s, which attacked Schweinfurt and Regensburg, with extremely heavy losses. Lastly, at the end of the year, the bombing raids on Berlin began. During 1943, no fewer than 135,000 tons of bombs were released on Germany, some of the heaviest raids being those carried out on Hamburg (11,000 tons), Essen (9,000 tons), and Cologne (8,000 tons).

The following year, the bombing raids were still further increased, and from February 1944, the new "double blow" technique was adopted for the first time. This consisted of a raid being repeated within a brief space of time on the same target. In the period between January 1 and June 5, 36 daytime raids and 102 night-time raids were carried out, affecting 37 cities, including Berlin (17 bombing raids), Braunschweig (13), Frankfurt-on-Main (8), Hannover, and Schweinfurt (5 raids). In the week of February 19-25 alone, the RAF and USAAF bombers dropped 16,700 tons of bombs on German aeronautical factories and airports. The quantity of bombs used in the course of the entire month was 38,000 tons (13,000 of which were released by the RAF). In March this figure rose to 55,000 tons (28,000 by the RAF), continuing to increase throughout April and May. Moreover, up till June 1, the bombing raids were carefully planned to prepare the ground for the Normandy landings.

The invasion kept the Allied aviation fully occupied. On June 6 alone, the units of the USAAF made almost 7,000 trips supporting the landings, releasing more than 3,600 tons of bombs. This activity also continued during the advance. However, the priority given to this task did not slow down the attacks on German territory. From mid-June, the principal targets became the refineries, in addition to the factories. The "double blow" tactic was increased, leading to three successful raids on the same target. The first cities to experience this were Munich (daytime raids, on July 11, 12, and 13) and Stuttgart (night-time raids, on July 24, 25, and 27). In the two months between June 6 and July 30, 1944, Germany was attacked for 18 days and nine nights. This frightening progression reached a peak during the first three months of 1945, when 329,000 tons of bombs were dropped on the Reich: 75,000 in January, 119,000 in February, and 135,000 in March. A summary of this final phase is provided by the following figures: from August 1, 1944 until April 1945, no fewer than 127 German cities were bombed, in 194 days and 94 nights; in the first four months of 1945, the raids numbered 404, 267 during the day and 137 at night.

Germany was by now on its last legs. On April 6, 1945, the RAF announced the suspension of British bombing raids on German territory, and four days later; following yet another raid on Berlin (the 420th since the beginning of the war), a similar decision was made by the USAAF. The strategic plans required that the forces be employed against the only adversary that still offered resistance: Japan.

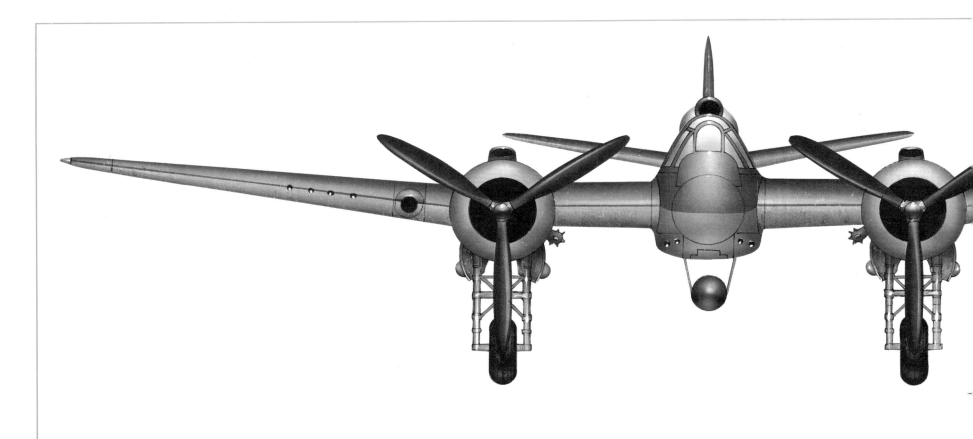

BRISTOL BEAUFIGHTER Mk.X

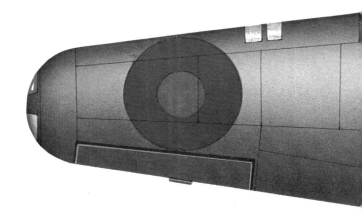

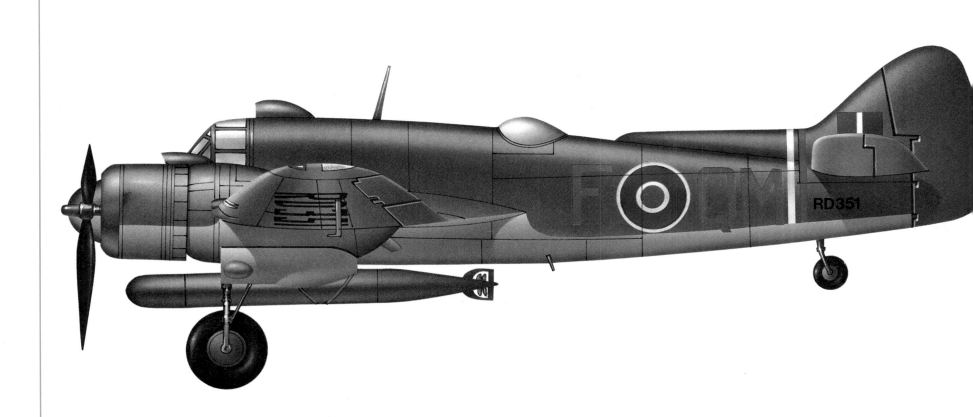

RD351

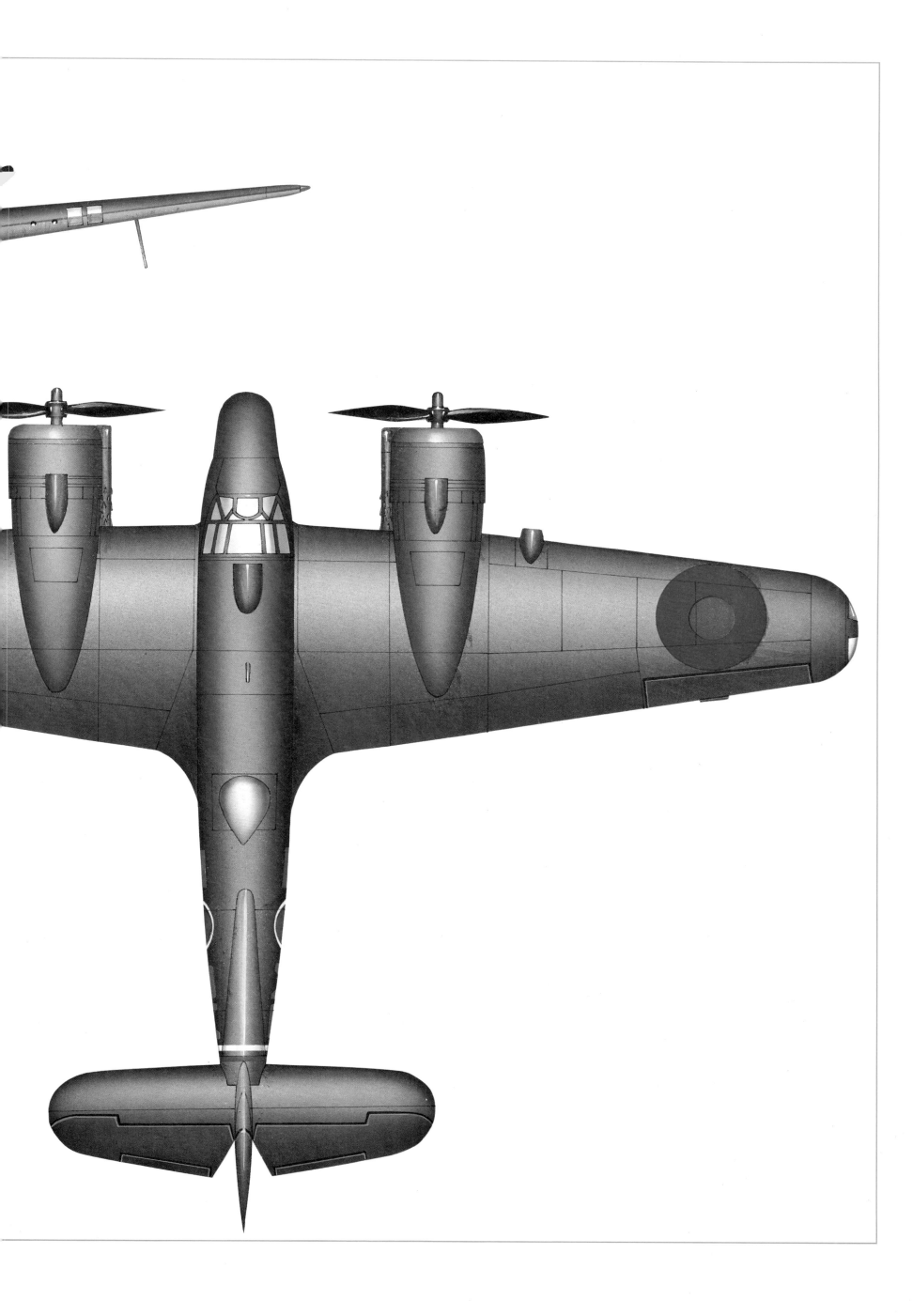

Although conceived back in 1938, the Bristol Beaufighter proved invincible in a great number of roles right until the end of the war. In fact, it served as a heavy fighter, night fighter, fighter-bomber, ground attack plane, torpedo plane, and in anti-submarine and anti-shipping attacks. The final version, the Mk.X, was prepared expressly for anti-shipping use. In all, 2,205 of this version were constructed and were intended almost exclusively for the units of the Royal Air Forces Coastal Command. They had started to use the Beaufighters in the spring of 1941, with the Mk.IC series. Their career became increasingly intensive with the use of the more powerful Mk.VICs of 1942, in which rockets and torpedoes were adopted for the first time. The combat missions of the Beaufighter torpedo planes (officially christened Torbeau) began in April 1943, and continued successfully for practically the entire duration of the conflict.

In 1943, these aircraft were joined by the first of the new variant. The Beaufighter Mk.X was fitted with XVII series Bristol Hercules radial engines (generating 1,795 hp), designed to supply maximum power at low altitudes. Its armament included virtually the entire range of weapons tested in the previous versions: rockets, a torpedo and bombs could be carried with equal ability and in various combinations. In addition, an AI Mk.VIII research radar was installed in the nose. However, the greater weight of the radar affected both its directional and longitudinal stability, and made it necessary to increase the balances' surface area and to fit the aircraft with a large fin on its back. Despite this, and thanks to the great firing power of the arms on board, the Mk.Xs proved to be deadly and an extremely efficient aircraft, especially against submarines. In March 1945, aircraft of the 236th and 254th Squadrons of Coastal Command located and destroyed no fewer than five German U-Boots within 48 hours. These Beaufighters had a particularly intensive career in northern Europe and the Mediterranean.

The last production series, designated Mk.XIC, also went to Coastal Command. These aircraft were basically Mk.Xs without torpedo launching equipment and 163 were completed. About 50 of them were supplied to the Royal Australian Air Force. Moreover, between 1944 and 1945, Australia built a further 364 on license, which were designated Beaufighter Mk.21. They carried out an important role in the Pacific: continuous attack missions against Japanese shipping.

In fact, it was in this role that the ''Beau'' earned perhaps the

A Beaufighter T.F.X. in flight over the North Sea.

most significant nick-name of its career: Whispering Death.

Another variant is also worthy of mention. Designated Mk.XII, it never went beyond the project phase: the aircraft's frame was notably reinforced, in order to allow an increase in the bomb load, while its power was entrusted to a pair of Bristol Hercules 27 radial engines.

color plate
Bristol Beaufighter Mk.X 254th Squadron - Coastal Command Royal Air Force - Great Britain 1943

Aircraft:	Bristol Beaufighter Mk.X
Nation:	Great Britain
Manufacturer:	Bristol Aeroplane Co. Ltd.
Type:	Fighter-bomber
Year:	1943
Engine:	2 Bristol Hercules XVII, 14-cylinder radial, air-cooled, 1,795 hp each
Wingspan:	57 ft 11 in (17.63 m)
Length:	41 ft 9 in (12.70 mm)
Height:	15 ft 10 in (4.83 m)
Weight:	25,231 lb (11,430 kg)
Maximum speed:	303 mph (488 km/h) at 1,315 ft (400 m)
Ceiling:	15,049 ft (4,575 m)
Range:	1,469 miles (2,367 km)
Armament:	4 x 20 mm cannons; 7 machine guns; 2,132 lb (966 kg) of bombs
Crew:	2

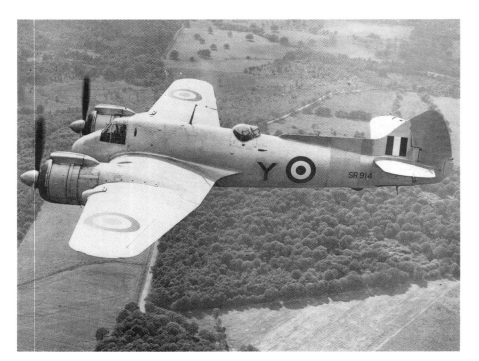
One of the last Beaufighter Mk.Xs to be built after the war. The tail fin of this aircraft is connected to the fuselage.

A Beaufighter during a rocket attack on German shipping targets.

CONTENTS